NEW YORK

THE SECRET ATLAS

T.M. Rives and Hannah Frishberg

JONGLEZ PUBLISHING

We have taken great pleasure in drawing up *New York – The Secret Atlas* and hope that through its guidance you will, like us, continue to discover unusual, hidden or little-known aspects of the city.

Descriptions of certain places are accompanied by thematic sections highlighting historical details or anecdotes as an aid to understanding the city in all its complexity.

This atlas also draws attention to the multitude of details found in places that we may pass every day without noticing.

It is an invitation to look more closely at the urban landscape and, more generally, a means of seeing our own city with the curiosity and attention that we often display while travelling elsewhere …

N
PASSAIC
CLEVELAND, DETROIT, CHICAGO ↑
80
80
280
280
ESSEX
95
95
NEW JERSEY
78
78
78
78
95
HUDSON
Newark Bay
Bridge
Newark
Jersey City
Newark
Bay
UNION
95
Goethals
Bridge
Bayonne
Bridge
278
278

WESTCHESTER
BERGEN
P. 204
George Washington Bridge
BRONX
Harlem
Randall's Island
P. 158
Hudson River
Central Park
Lincoln Tunnel
La Guardia
P. 172
Queensboro Bridge
P. 108
NEW YORK
MANHATTAN
Midtown
P. 132
QUEENS
Queens Midtown Tunnel
Flushing Meadows
P. 70
River
Holland Tunnel
Ellis Island
Downtown
P. 48
Brooklyn Heights
Governors Island
NEW YORK
P. 14
Liberty Island
Upper Bay
Prospect Park
BROOKLYN
John F. Kennedy
KINGS
Verrazano-Narrows Bridge
Jamaica Bay

BELOW CHAMBERS

CHAMBERS TO HOUSTON

HOUSTON TO 14TH

FROM 14TH TO 42ND

FROM 42ND TO 59TH

UPPER WEST SIDE (59TH – 110TH)

UPPER EAST SIDE AND CENTRAL PARK

UPPER MANHATTAN

BELOW CHAMBERS

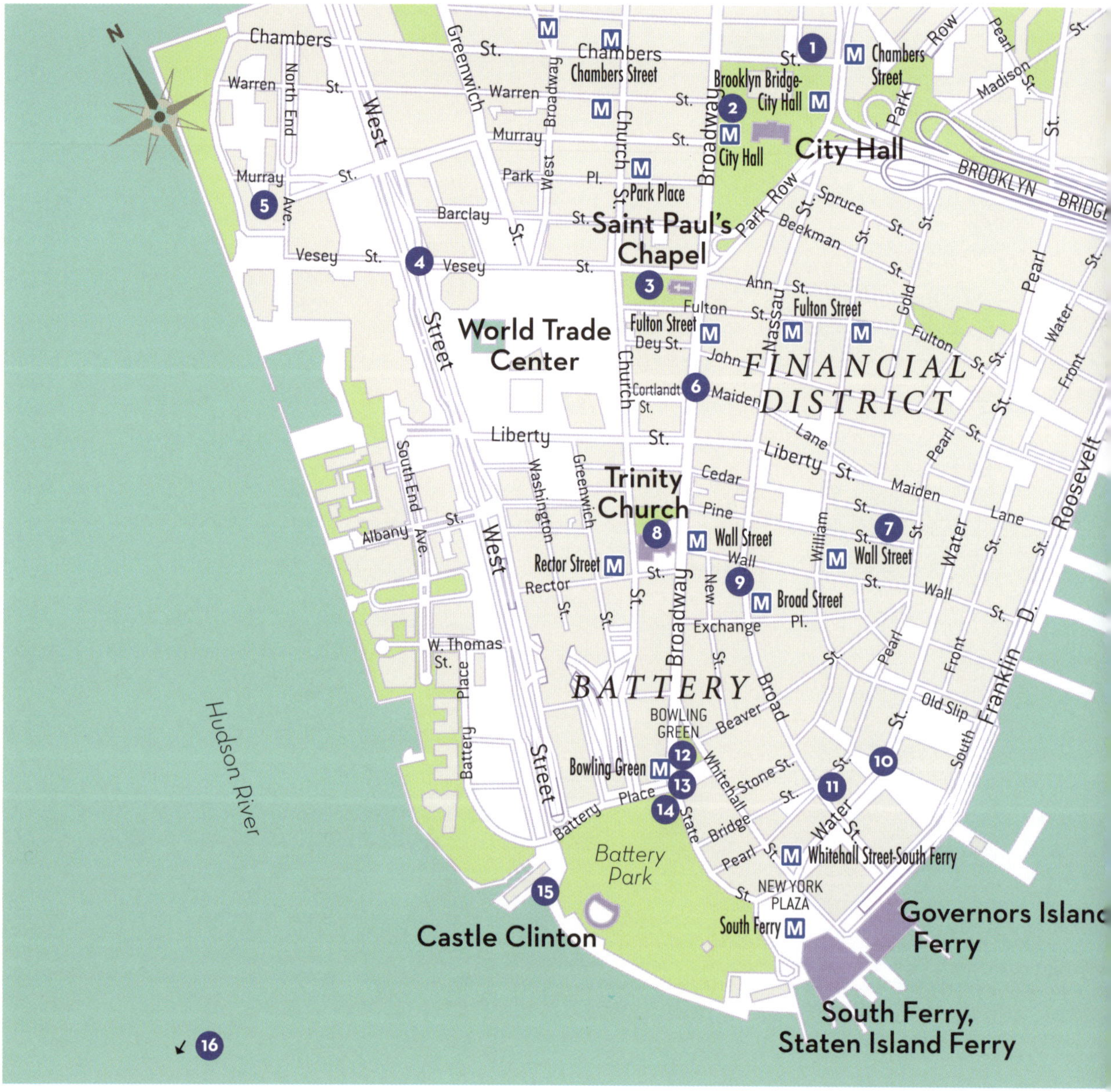

10. ELEVATED ACRE *p. 34*

11. GEORGE WASHINGTON'S TOOTH *p. 36*

12. THE FENCE AT BOWLING GREEN *p. 38*

13. BELGIUM ON THE CUSTOMS HOUSE *p. 40*

14. NETHERLANDS MONUMENT FLAGPOLE *p. 42*

15. AMERICAN MERCHANT MARINERS' MEMORIAL *p. 44*

16. GRAFFITI COLUMNS OF ELLIS ISLAND *p. 46*

01.

31 Chambers Street
J and Z trains/Chambers Street
4, 5 and 6 trains/Brooklyn Bridge – City Hall

CITY SEALS OF THE SURROGATE'S COURT

New York's history in symbols

The city is full of examples of the official seal, but few New Yorkers could describe it to you. Seals are like currency: rich in symbols and so common few notice the details. They're also windows into the past. One of the best places to plot the city's history through seals is the Surrogate's Court Building, in the spandrels of the three arches over the entrance.

The seals are in chronological order. On the far right you see a European man and an Algonquin Indian flanking a heraldic shield. The European holds a sounding line – a lead weight attached to a rope to measure water depth – indicating that he's a sailor, a nod to the colonization of the New World by sea and New York's importance as a maritime hub. The Indian holds a single-curve bow and wears feathers behind his head – both Algonquin style. In the center of the shield is a large X: the blades of a windmill. Between the blades are the beavers that interested early settlers for their pelts – the foundation of New York's wealth and the sole reason for settling the place to begin with – and barrels of flour, a staple that the city monopolized and grew rich from in its early history. Above hangs a half-globe topped with a cocky American eagle.

Interesting, now, to roll back through history to the left. In the next seal the eagle is gone and in its place is the pre-Revolution imperial crown of Britain. The date on the bottom, 1686, marks the year New York was granted a city charter. One more step to the left and we are back in the New Amsterdam of the Dutch; the beaver now basks atop the seal of old Amsterdam. Notice here where the windmill's X came from: repeating saltire crosses in the heraldry of that city. And back one last time: the seal of New Netherland, with the long-suffering beaver and, circling the shield, a string of Indian wampum, two forms of local currency in the earliest days of colonization when New York was just a collection of adventuring outcasts on a marshy island, barely an idea let alone a city.

The Surrogate's Court Building was finished before 1915, when New York's official seal was drawn up. You can find the up-todate version inside on the security guard's podium. Other modern official seals appear on the city flag, on the arm patches of police officers, and behind the health inspection rating in the window of nearly every restaurant.

02.

City Hall, on Broadway between Murray and Warren Streets
N and R trains/City Hall
2 and 3 trains/Park Place
J and Z trains/Chambers Street
4, 5 and 6 trains/Brooklyn Bridge – City Hall

THE LIBERTY POLE

First blood of the Revolution

Perhaps due to the city's long habit of destroying its own past, the crucial role New York played in the Revolution has been strangely subdued in the American imagination. New York was the key to military advantage and the British knew it: taking the city meant splitting the Colonies in half. George Washington knew it too: the first battles were fought in Boston, but when the British were beaten there, the next place the general rushed to defend was this one. Most Americans are surprised to learn that the first blood spilled in the conflict – before the Boston Massacre, and long before the pitched battles of 1776 – was likely spilled downtown. What's more, there's a reminder of it at City Hall: the Liberty Pole.

There were liberty poles in many American cities before and during the Revolution. From an idea originating in Boston's Liberty Tree (an elm where dissenters gathered), they were essentially flagstaffs planted in the ground. New York's pole became the symbol of discord for both sides: the Sons of Liberty kept raising it, and the British kept knocking it down.

On December 16, 1769, an anti-British broadside was circulated to the "Betrayed Inhabitants of the City." It spoke of Tyranny and Despotism, among other fighting words, and was signed "A Son of Liberty." This was too much for the British. Soldiers from the Sixteenth Regiment blew the pole up with charges of gunpowder, sawed it to pieces, and printed a broadside of their own blasting the "real enemies of society" who "thought their freedom depended on a piece of wood." Redcoats hung the insult all over town.

Collectors of bizarre historical trivia will be pleased that a ram's horn, of all things, played a role in what followed. On January 19, 1770, New York merchant and patriot Isaac Sears and his friend Walter Quackenbos nabbed a pair of British soldiers posting the offensive broadside. There was a scuffle; when bayonets came out, Sears, who happened to have a ram's horn in his hand, got the idea to throw it at one of the soldiers' heads. Support swarmed to both sides, and in the Battle of Golden Hill on present-day John Street several men were wounded and one patriot killed.

Afterward an 80-foot pine mast was sunk deep into private land next to the Common and girded in iron. At the top, as on the one you can see at City Hall today, was a golden vane bearing a single word: LIBERTY.

LIBERTY

03.

Saint Paul's Chapel
209 Broadway
trinitywallstreet.org/about/stpaulschapel
A,C, 2, 3, 4 and 5 trains/Broadway – Nassau Street
E train/Chambers Street
6 train/Brooklyn Bridge – City Hall

THE CROWN ON ST. PAUL'S PULPIT

The last surviving royal symbol in New York

St. Paul's Chapel, completed in 1766, is the oldest standing church in Manhattan. Inside you'll find the bench where George Washington attended service, and above it hangs the first known full-color seal of the United States. These relics, along with the fact that Washington prayed here after his inauguration a few blocks south on Wall Street, makes St. Paul's something like the most American church in the country. But one small detail reveals the chapel's – and the city's – colonial past: the pulpit and sounding board (both original) are topped by a white coronet. In all of New York, it's likely the only symbol of British rule that survived the tumult of the Revolution.

The colonial governors got their first taste of an angry New York mob in 1765 during the riots against the hated Stamp Act. But this was just a warm-up for the wreckage that took place after the reading of the Declaration of Independence.

New York's Provincial Congress assented on July 9, 1776, and at 6 o'clock the document that announced America's rupture with the Kingdom of Great Britain was read aloud to troops in the Common (today City Hall Park). The reaction was...spirited. "My Lord," wrote the colonial governor William Tryon to the British Secretary of State, "The confederate Colonies have declared themselves independent States: Enclosed is a copy of their Declaration of Independency, which was published through the streets of New York in the middle of last month, where the King's Statue has been demolished, as well as the King's Arms in the City Hall, the established churches shut up, & every Vistage of Royalty, as far as has been in the power of the Rebels, done away."

The "Vistage of Royalty" that was most famously done away with was the King George statue and the finials of the iron gate surrounding Bowling Green (see page 38); for a tactile connection with history, run your hand over the uneven tops of the posts: some are still rough from where the hack saws cut the crowns off. The royal coronet on the top of the pulpit of St. Paul's presumably survived when the chapel was shuttered against the ecstatic vandals.

04.

Three World Financial Center
Corner of Vesey and West Street
1, 2 and 3 trains/Chambers St or Park Place
A and C trains/Chambers Street
E train/ World Trade Center

THE HARBORS OF THE WORLD

One of the largest mural cycles ever painted

Three World Financial Center, also known as the American Express Tower, places New York in the context of global maritime trade with one of the largest mural cycles ever painted, Craig McPherson's *Harbors of the World*. The work wraps around all four sides of the tower lobby: linen panels 11 feet high, with a combined width of 318 feet. This sounds big. It looks bigger. Just as photographs can't capture the paintings' scale and atmosphere, neither, as McPherson explained in an interview, can they capture a harbor landscape in the wild. "Forms fall away too quickly and the base line curves," he said, "among other distortions." The artist adopted his own method of perspective using surveying equipment, spending months at a carefully chosen vantage for each scene. The harbors were selected for prominence, diversity, and topography. In addition to New York, there are lustrous and subtly textured panoramas of Venice, Istanbul, Hong Kong, Sydney, and Rio de Janeiro.

Assistants transferred the drawings to stretched linen and did a first pass of grey tints, but McPherson alone, working at a rate of 10 feet per month, did all the painting. Each city has an individual color scheme and feel: Venice is moody, Hong Kong shimmers in furtive blue-greens, Sydney is bright.

Like every building in this neighborhood, Three World Financial Center has a dramatic 9/11 story. Glass and debris tumbled onto the floor where the murals hang, and the Winter Garden on the bay side of the complex was half-buried in smoking girders. A grinning guard notes that, although the murals were unharmed, in the one featuring New York – a glowing skyline at night – the Twin Towers seem to be engulfed in prophetic flame.

New York is considered the finest natural harbor on the Atlantic Ocean – perhaps the finest anywhere. Sandy Hook and Rockaway Point provide protection from the ocean; from there the Verrazano Narrows calm the waters even further into the Upper Bay where the Hudson River debouches from New York State's deep interior. This arrangement was the key to the city's success; the port and finance were two sides of the same coin until well into the 20th century.

05.

290 Vesey Street
A and C trains/Chambers Street
N and R trains/City Hall
2 and 3 trains/Park Place

IRISH HUNGER MEMORIAL

All of Ireland hidden above the street

"We stop the Press, with very great regret, to announce that the Potato Murrain has unequivocally declared itself in Ireland." So reads the Gardeners' Chronicle of September, 1845. The word "murrain" literally means "death;" the fungus-like organism that causes potato blight is microscopic, but within ten years it had wiped out a large part of Ireland's population.

More than a million died of hunger; twice that many emigrated. The disaster, with its themes of nostalgia and displacement, is summarized at the Irish Hunger Memorial in Battery Park City.

There are several spots in New York that create the illusion, often in a very tight space, that you're no longer in the city. The better Vest Pocket parks (see page 164) are based on this idea. The Hunger Memorial doctors the scenery more completely than any corner of New York. Here you aren't just transported to a vague "somewhere else" – you're transported specifically to Ireland.

Passers-by who see the monument only from the ground have little idea that, cantilevered 25 feet above their heads, are the ruins of a Famine-era cottage and a path winding through wild grass and along stone walls. All the plants here are Irish natives; scattered about are rugged boulders gathered from all thirty-two Irish counties. Crouch down in the blackthorn and foxglove

© CTA ARCHITECTS

next to a piece of Limerick or Kilkenny and you can see nothing but Ireland, and sky. Stand up and you can see the Statue of Liberty.

In the limestone tunnel that leads up to the memorial, selections of writing about the Great Famine remind visitors about the misery it caused. There's a list of plants that Ireland's poor ate when the potatoes turned black: nettles, dandelion, tree leaves.

During the mass emigration, New York's population became a quarter Irish, most of them desperate. "Foreigners," reads one anti-immigration banner from the period, "are paupers, strangers, sojourners, loafers, and other cattle" – words that have been used by some to describe every wave of immigrants since.

It took years for Irish Americans to beat the stigma of Catholicism, poverty, and crime. By 1860 the flood of immigrants had abated. A century later John F. Kennedy was elected president.

Today New York can still claim more Irish-Americans than any other city in the United States.

06.

Clock: corner of Maiden Lane and Broadway
William Barthman Jewelers: 176 Broadway
williambarthman.com
4 and 5 trains/Fulton Street
N and R trains/Cortlandt Street
A, C, J and Z trains/Fulton Street

SIDEWALK CLOCK ON MAIDEN LANE

Time ticking underfoot

William Barthman Jewelers on Broadway is the last holdout of a buzzing lower Manhattan jewelry trade that started in the late 1700s. The store has been on the same block for 130 years, a record of service you can see in the historic photos hanging inside, and feel in the unstrained courtesy of the staff behind the counters. But the store's most inspired public relations move was the sidewalk clock on the corner of Maiden Lane. "People know us by that clock," says Connie, the manager.

Founder William Barthman tweaked the concept of sponsored city clocks by placing his underfoot. The sidewalk seems alive on that corner; the glass crystal and the steadily advancing hands bravely submit to endless stomping pedestrians (50,000 in a three-hour period, according to one count).

Regularly serviced and synched, the clock is kept going by an electric motor that had to be replaced after 9/11. Guilo, the Barthman's bench jeweler, points out a thin crack in the sidewalk that scribbles from the east to contact the bronze setting at the Roman numeral twelve. "September 11 was like a little earthquake," he says. "The clock is safe because of the caulking, but there's still some water leaking." Connie has a placid outlook. "I think it'll be there long after we're gone."

There are screws around the setting that secure the timepiece to the sidewalk but, surprisingly, the way to get to the mechanism is from underneath. Guilo opens a door on Maiden Lane and leads the way down a hot stairwell to a rare tour of the deeper history of Barthman's: dust, the guts of the HVAC, and wooden cabinets with files going back a century.

Under the clock is a small workspace and a desk bristling with tools for cutting, filing, and polishing fine jewelry. Guilo removes a piece of corrugated plastic in the ceiling, and, with pride, reveals the clock's underside.

Daylight bleeds around the rim, flickering to the muted tick-tock of heels on the sidewalk overhead. When the 6 train goes by just a few feet on the other side of the concrete wall, everything rumbles.

Back on street level, two cashiers at the vitamin store on the corner who stand not 10 feet from the old clock say they've never noticed it before. "I must have stepped on it a million times," says one. "But that's New York – you get jaded. Hey, put that in the book."

WILLIAM
E
BARTHMAN
S
1884
W
SINCE
N

07.

70 Pine Street
2 and 3 trains/Wall Street

SCALE MODEL AT THE AMERICAN INTERNATIONAL BUILDING

An overlooked Titan

One test of greatness in skyscrapers is if an image of the building can be tastefully included in the decoration. New York's three most famous skyscrapers carry it off: the Woolworth, the Chrysler, and the Empire State Buildings all have depictions of themselves in the murals and details of their lobbies.

The Woolworth tells its whole story in stone carvings, including the architect holding the building in miniature, and retail magnate Frank W. Woolworth himself (who began his career as a stock boy) carefully counting coins.

The American International Building on Pine Street took the practice to a new level with the brazen inclusion of a 12-foot version of its own self, carved in stone and to correct scale, on both the north and south facades. At the bottom the stone replica even features a still tinier version: the scale model of the model. This attention might seem out of place in a building most New Yorkers couldn't name, but you can argue that the AIB belongs among the ranks of the skyscraper legends mentioned above. Upon completion it became the tallest building downtown (and regained the title after 9/11); the style is drop-jaw Gothic; snowy mountains are evoked in the white stone of the tower's peak, where an open-air platform offered an unrivaled view of downtown and the Upper Bay. The famous elevators were double-decker, operated by beautiful redheads recruited, according to one account, "from the ranks of unemployed showgirls" – which, with your choice of hair color, apparently weren't lacking during the Depression. What happened? Why didn't the AIB take hold in the public imagination?

Maybe New York was just exhausted. The AIB was begun in 1930, two years into the frenzied "skyscraper race" for the world's tallest building, where the Chrysler competed against the Bank of Manhattan Building (and pipped it at the tape by concealing the addition of a 125-foot spire) until both were creamed by the Empire State in 1931. The finished AIB was likewise taller than the Bank of Manhattan Building – but by then it hardly mattered. The race was over.

Today the Empire State still reigns supreme. For seventy-five years the AIB had the sour title of tallest building in New York that was never the tallest building in the world; that, too, was taken away in 2007 by the New York Times Building. It's still the only skyscraper with the dash to have its own self chiseled proudly over the entrance.

08.

Trinity Cemetery
74 Trinity Place (Broadway at Wall Street)
trinitywallstreet.org
1, N and R trains/Rector Street
4 and 5 trains/Wall Street

TRINITY'S TOMBSTONE RIDDLE

Coded messages from the dead

The oldest tombstone you can find in Trinity Church cemetery is that of Richard Churcher, who died in 1681 at the age of 5. The boy has a small, sturdy stone that is curious for being double-sided: on the back is a carving in high-relief of an hourglass with wings, and below it a skull-and-crossbones.

The message is unmistakable: time flies, and then – *poof*. Some paces away, near the Soldier's Monument at the graveyard's north end, you'll find the stone of James Leeson, a man who died more than a hundred years later. The winged hourglass is chiseled here as well, along with Masonic symbols. But above these, following the stone's natural curve, is a message in a devious code that took nearly a century to crack.

The code takes the form of partial squares. The squares either contain dots – sometimes one, sometimes two – or remain empty. The key to the solution is knowing why the squares are missing sides: they're really just boxes in a tic-tac-toe grid. The dots mark different stages in the alphabet, jumping the letter "j" because it was interchangeable with "i" at the time.

The code freights the message with grandeur, whatever it actually says. Are these last words to a secret lover? Location of a treasure? A zero-calorie apple cobbler recipe?

Disappointingly, the message simply spells REMEMBER DEATH. Why James Leeson took such elaborate pains to conceal a sentiment that can be conveyed neatly (and wordlessly) in a symbol – in fact the only sentiment that absolutely no one who ever entered a cemetery really needs pointed out in the first place – is a mystery. But since the message wasn't for us, we can't complain. The code system is known as a pigpen cipher, which also goes by the name "Freemason's cipher." For what it's worth, Leeson's buddies would have understood.

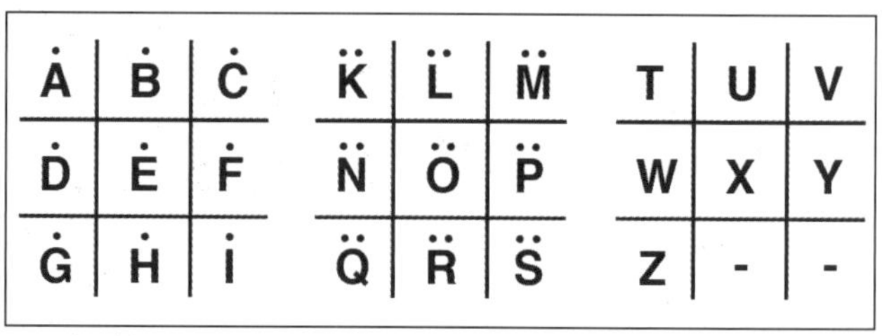

Key to the riddle

Here lies
depofited the Body of
James Leefon
Life
1794

09.

23 Wall Street
2 and 3 trains/Wall Street

BLAST MARKS ON THE MORGAN BANK

A scar on Wall Street

At lunchtime on September 16, 1920, a horse-drawn wagon clopped down Wall Street and halted in front of the J.P. Morgan & Company Bank headquarters. The wagon was so ordinary, witnesses later couldn't agree on a description. Inside was a cargo that would rattle history: a timer detonator, jagged slugs of metal, and a load of explosives, probably dynamite. While the bells of nearby Trinity Church were tolling noon, the timer went off.

"I was lifted completely off the ground," a messenger later said, "the terrific force of concussion blowing my hat off my head." The shock wave shook the glass from skyscrapers three blocks away. A reporter for the *Sun & New York Herald* described the scene in language chillingly evocative of another, more recent disaster: "It was a crash out of a blue sky, an unexpected, death-dealing bolt which in a twinkling turned into a shambles the busiest corner of America's financial center." The horse was atomized: its hooves were later found near Trinity Cemetery.

There were 38 dead in all, and hundreds injured, making the Wall Street explosion the worst terrorist bombing in the U.S. until Oklahoma City (1995), and the worst in New York until 9/11. A force of government agencies scrutinized clues and conducted countless interviews in a three-year investigation that stretched all the way to Russia. In the end the bomber was never identified, nor was the group, if any, he belonged to. It's unlikely he was a solitary lunatic: the early 1900s was a period of fire and blood, a battle between capital and labor, and any adult in 1920 could list a number of recent attacks against symbols of American authority: assassination attempts on the President, mail bombs, dynamite on railroads and in factories. Today most people are amazed to learn that the Wall Street explosion ever took place, but forgetting about it is practically a tradition. On the fifth anniversary of the bombing, a *Wall Street Journal* reporter found that passing office workers didn't know why the marble wall of the Morgan Bank was scarred with pockmarks – marks that are still visible today. "How quickly," he wrote, "time effaces the memory of startling events."

10.

Entrance at 55 Water Street
N and R trains/Whitehall Street
J and Z trains/Broad Street
2 and 3 trains/Wall Street

ELEVATED ACRE

Unexpected stillness

It takes a skewed relationship with nature for a city to exalt a small rectangle of plain grass. That's the situation at lower Manhattan's Elevated Acre.

The name alone has a worshipful resonance; the secret patch of green might be all that's between the more sensitive of the Financial District office crowd and total melancholy. When the sun is strong, the grass seems a little like a trick, as though at any moment it could shimmer and dissolve into the ugly roof the city wants it to be. It doesn't matter exactly how much nature has been tucked away here, or how many people are enjoying it (in the morning it could be zero) or that the grass is actually permanently emerald astroturf. The attraction is the pleasure in seeing urban traits – height, geometry, modernity – aligned with the concept of the humble lawn. It's marvelous or terrible, depending on your mood.

You enter at the widest, most heavily trafficked section of Water Street, where the buildings are all corporate titans. You ride to the green on a long clean escalator that promises open sky up ahead. The south part of the acre has islands of plants that divide it into more or less private spaces: whatever your neurosis, you'll find a spot to suit you. On the north end are tiered cement steps or seats that lead down to the holy lawn. This is where office workers peering down from the surrounding glass skyscrapers are gladdened and saddened to see sunbathers in the summer, and where you could have a harrowing game of Frisbee. To savor the effect, stand near the rail that keeps you from plunging a couple of stories down into Old Slip: the sight of lawn above and busy street below is truly odd.

But perhaps the best reason to come to the Elevated Acre is the view in the other direction. You can see all of Brooklyn Heights across the East River, down to the cranes of Red Hook. Upriver stretch the Brooklyn and Manhattan Bridges; downriver is Governor's Island. The constant hum of cars speeding on East River Drive and the choppers chuffing at the heliport might annoy you if you seek only peace, but at the rail, looking over the windy river you'll appreciate the acre for what it is: relative stillness in the general whirl.

11.

Fraunces Tavern, 54 Pearl Street
fraunces tavernmuseum.org
N and R trains/Whitehall Street
4 and 5 trains/Bowling Green
1 train/South Ferry

GEORGE WASHINGTON'S TOOTH

Odd relics in Fraunces Tavern

Fraunces Tavern, established in 1762, still operates a restaurant and bar on the ground floor. The upstairs has been turned into a museum where you can get a large and personal dose of the Revolutionary War – paintings, arms, newspaper clippings, diaries – as well as see two natural objects that are as rare as they are odd: a lock of George Washington's hair, and a piece of one of his teeth.

The tavern bills itself as "the oldest surviving structure in Manhattan" but very little is original. What you see is a faithful restoration completed in 1907, after the building was saved from demolition (the owners wanted to flatten it for a parking lot). Lucky: the tavern is a direct line to post-colonial New York. The address was briefly Washington's last residence as general of the American Revolutionary forces, and he made here his farewell speech to officers at the war's end in 1783.

The building's importance goes deeper: in a city that suddenly became the capital of a newly-minted nation, the tavern was used as offices for the first Department of War, as well as Treasury and Foreign Affairs.

The so-called Long Room – site of the farewell – has been preserved to look just as it did on December 4, 1783. In an account by intelligence officer Benjamin Tallmadge, who was present, Washington raised a glass, expressed "a heart full of love and gratitude," and took his formal leave. Tallmadge's diary, permanently opened to the section containing the scene, is on display.

One wonders how Washington would have felt about fragments of his person being offered on display as well. "The first thing people ask," says the young man at the museum ticket counter, "is when we can make a clone of him."

The body relics are in a glass case. The tooth, hard to see, is mounted in a pendant; the hair, a surprisingly virile chestnut (Americans might be forgiven for believing that Washington was born with white curls) rests in a round frame. The tooth is a little creepy for being a fragment, as though at death Washington were carefully slivered up like the true cross, but the first president's dental woes are legendary. When he took the oath of office (only a few blocks away on Wall Street) he had only one tooth left. Clinging to it was a frightening contraption made of hippo ivory, gold, human teeth, and spiral springs.

Tooth fragment
Dr. John Greenwood
United States, 1789-1798
Contrary to American legend, Washington's
dentures were composed of animal and human
teeth, not wood. Dr. John Greenwood made
five separate sets for Washington who seems to

12.

Bowling Green Park
4 and 5 trains/Bowling Green

THE FENCE AT BOWLING GREEN

One of the oldest structures in Manhattan

Bowling Green, located at the very end of Broadway, is the oldest park in New York City. The circular green is also the site of the most ironic episode of the Revolutionary War.

In 1765, the Stamp Act went into effect. The act was a way for the British to fund their military by requiring all official colonial business to use stamped paper. The measure was simple, self-enforcing, and in retrospect not too smart: the rage it sparked was the colonists' first step toward open revolt. Here in New York the response was characteristically unsubtle: the royal governor's carriage was set afire, and an effigy of the man was hanged and burned right here in Bowling Green.

After the act was repealed, things calmed down. In 1770 the British again showed questionable foresight when they delivered a 4,000-pound equestrian statue of King George III. The statue, paid for by New Yorkers and placed in the center of the green, was made of gilt lead. The gilding was a nice touch; the lead, as will be seen, was a bad idea.

New Yorkers will be cheered to know that graffiti and vandalism have a long history in the city. As tensions rose, the statue was so abused a cast-iron fence had to be built around it.

On July 9, 1776, the Declaration of Independence was read for the first time in New York on the Common (City Hall Park today), and a mob of civilians and soldiers with liberty fever stormed the fence and tore the statue down.

As King George was being dashed to pieces, some inspired rebel observed that a 4,000-pound lead equestrian statue could probably be melted down into quite a lot of bullets. The exact count came to 44,088. The number of Redcoats killed by a hot flying plug of King George is unknown.

Parts of the statue, as well as the marble slab it rested on, are now kept at the New York Historical Society.

The fence is still right here. It's been keeping the roaring city at bay for coming on two and a half centuries, and is one of the oldest structures in Manhattan.

BOWLING
GREEN

13.

1 Bowling Green
4 and 5 trains/Bowling Green
1 train/South Ferry
R train/Whitehall Street
M, J and Z trains/Broad Street

BELGIUM ON THE CUSTOMS HOUSE

A Belgium allegory that was once Germany

You generally don't get to see modern geopolitical tensions written out in city architecture, but the U.S. Customs House on Bowling Green has an odd case of exactly that. High above, on the attic level, stand 12 marble statues representing the great seagoing powers of the world. One of them is ... Belgium. Belgium, you might know, has only about 40 miles of coastline. Here's the story.

The Customs House (now the New York branch of the National Museum of the American Indian) was designed in 1900 to be the most impressive building in the city. The entire world's commerce flowed through this address, and the theme of international trade is permanently fixed in the statuary.

On the lower level are female allegories of the four continents by Daniel Chester French; above are sculpted heads of Mercury, the Roman god of trade, and portraits of the "eight races of mankind."

From the cornice the 12 great seagoing powers, both historical and modern, strike regal poses. Belgium is third from right. With Portugal and Denmark on one side, and France and England on the other, she's outclassed. The reason: the Belgium allegory was once Germany. After the start of World War I it was decided that a hostile enemy had no place on a government building, and Treasury Secretary William McAdoo asked the sculptor to transform Germany into Belgium. The secretary was unbothered by the fact that Belgium didn't have a navy at the time: she was a U.S. ally, dammit.

Here the story gets even more interesting. Half a dozen different sculptors had worked on the allegories; Germany was the only one sculpted by a native German. Albert Jaegers, an American citizen who had moved from Europe as a boy, was an accomplished artist and favorite for German subjects. When the Treasury Secretary asked him to mar his own work, he refused. The kind of people who get hysterical over this sort of thing immediately got hysterical. Jaegers' refusal was attributed to a latent loyalty to the Kaiser, who had once given the artist a decoration. Called before the National Sculpture Society, Jaegers made the point that the statue's identity couldn't be altered by "a little camouflage with a relabel." No matter: he was widely vilified, the lady was scoured of national insignia, and BELGIUM was chiseled into her shield.

BELGIUM

14.

North end of Battery Park,
where Battery Place meets State Street
nycgovparks.org/parks/batterypark/highlights/8094
4 and 5 trains/Bowling Green

NETHERLANDS MONUMENT FLAGPOLE

Twenty-four dollars worth of beads

On December 7, 1926, the Netherland-America Foundation presided over a ceremony in Battery Park. It was so cold hardly anyone showed up; the members of the brass band huddled in taxi cabs. The occasion was the 300th anniversary of the settlement of Manhattan by the Dutch, and to mark it, a large pink stone flagpole base was unveiled: carved by a Dutchman, and paid for by the good people of Holland. You can still see it today.

If people know only one story about New York history, it's usually the one depicted here: the famed Sale of Manhattan, where the early Dutch settlers buy the whole island from the Indians for a handful of beads worth $24. The legend is savory to New Yorkers: it's about a lopsided property deal where the forward-thinking party wins and the rube loses his shirt. But the legend is wrong, as summed up in a single detail on the pink flagpole: the Indian's war bonnet. It's a mistake you'll find in public images throughout the city. War bonnets were worn by Plains Indians, never by Algonquins. Some might say it's a small thing, but it's a small thing that makes room for everything else.

For instance, there is no document of sale for Manhattan at all. There's a document of sale for Staten Island, and that's where the idea of the fistful of beads came from. Perhaps Manhattan was sold for what Staten Island went for – tools, cloth, wampum – but the legend spotlights those beads, as though the dull Indian was baffled by a gewgaw into throwing away his birthright. "Our people are in good spirit and live in peace," reads a Dutch letter, the only record of the exchange. "They have purchased the Island of Manhattes from the savages for the value of 60 guilders." That's all we know. The exchange for 60 guilders has been forever fixed at $24.

But what's a dollar? The Native American notions of money, not to mention land ownership, were inscrutable to Europeans. To illustrate, the Dutch had to "buy" Staten Island a total of five times. For the Indian, the "sale of Manhattan" was likely at most the "rent of Manhattan" – or he might have been taking goods for land he had no tribal connection with at all. There's reason to think that the Lenape who sold Manhattan returned home chuckling that these pasty, short, soft-bellied seafarers stinking of animal waste and cheese had traveled so far just to get swindled.

15.

Battery Park, just northwest of Castle Clinton
nycgovparks.org
4 and 5 trains/Bowling Green
1 train/South Ferry
N and R trains/Whitehall Street

AMERICAN MERCHANT MARINERS' MEMORIAL

All hands!

Out on a stone breakwater, bronze sailors huddle on the deck of a sinking boat. One tries to save a companion who reaches from the lapping waves; another cups his hands to shout for help. The American Merchant Mariners' Memorial has such dramatic immediacy because – strange among monuments – it's based on a photograph. This photograph has its own rich story of contingency and adventure, and at the center of it all is a man whose name appears nowhere at the memorial. George W. Duffy was barely 20 when, in September 1942, his American merchant vessel was sunk by a German cruiser off South Africa. The survivors were transferred to an enemy supply ship where they languished for a month. While leafing through the Berliner Illustrierte Zeitung, Duffy came across a story about a torpedoed U.S. oil tanker; with the story was a photo of seven men in a life raft whom Duffy immediately recognized as fellow merchant seamen. Believing that later they'd be amused by the photo, "and naively thinking," he wrote, "the war would not last very long," he tore the page out and kept it.

Duffy and the other prisoners were turned over to the Japanese. For the next three years – in Java, Singapore, Sumatra – he lived in camps until he was liberated, along with other "walking skeletons," by the British in 1945. All the while, the magazine photo remained stashed in his gear. "After the war," he wrote, "I took this page to as many of the oil tanker companies as I could find in New York. No one could identify the seven men." And so the matter rested for forty years when, in the early 1980s, a historian had the photo analyzed by the FBI. By enhancing a life vest, the name of the merchantmen's ship was made visible for the first time: Muskogee. The photo had been taken by a German journalist from the very submarine that had blown the oil tanker out of the water. The shouting sailors captured on film are the last portraits of dead men: records show the Muskogee lost all hands. "All hands!" wrote Duffy. "And for all those years I had been searching for living survivors."

French-born sculptor Marisol used Duffy's photograph to sketch the monument. It was dedicated in 1991.

16.

Ellis Island
Ferry tickets available at Castle Clinton in Battery Park
nps.gov/elis/index.htm

GRAFFITI COLUMNS OF ELLIS ISLAND

The other immigrants

The traditional narrative of Ellis Island is one-way: the Statue of Liberty raises her torch to welcome incoming traffic from afar.

You rarely hear about traffic going in the *other* direction: the folks who made it here – also after feats of daring and sacrifice – but ended up getting kicked out again. You can come strangely close to the lives of these other people on the third floor of the main building, just above the great Registry Room. There you'll find two columns that are covered, on all sides and from top to bottom, with penciled graffiti.

Barry Moreno is a librarian and historian at Ellis Island, and author of *The Encyclopedia of Ellis Island* and *The Statue of Liberty Encyclopedia*. He can see the columns from his desk. "The story the tourists get," he says, "is of the thousands of immigrants coming into Ellis Island every day off the ships – the massive immigration. And that story is the major story. But it happened between 1892 and 1924."

In 1921 the American government began enforcing immigration quotas; between then and World War II, Ellis Island became a universal detention center for unwanted aliens. "You had prostitutes," says Moreno, "ex-convicts, down-and-outs, vagrants. People who had been in hospital or orphanages, people who suffered from insanity or epilepsy. Alcoholics..."

Some of these people had been living in the States for years; many even crossed over from Mexico or Canada before the borders were enforced. Generally they got arrested for some crime – in Seattle, Kansas City, Chicago – and, when they couldn't prove legal entry, were packed onto trains. "The train would wind up in New York," says Moreno, "and all of the detainees – hundreds of them – would be brought under guard to Ellis Island."

Just beyond the columns was the Special Inquiry Division, where deportation cases were investigated. Unlike arriving immigrants, who were processed and ejected into the city in a matter of hours, detainees were stuck waiting. To relieve the tedium, and to rebel, and to leave some trace of themselves in the country that had refused them, they would scribble on the walls. There are cartoons of officials, and animals, and faces, and tender portraits of women. One man seemed to want to defend his legitimate entry into America, offering a testimony – in Italian: "Cecchini, Giuseppe," his message reads. "Arrived at the Battery on Saturday, May 18, 1901."

CHAMBERS TO HOUSTON

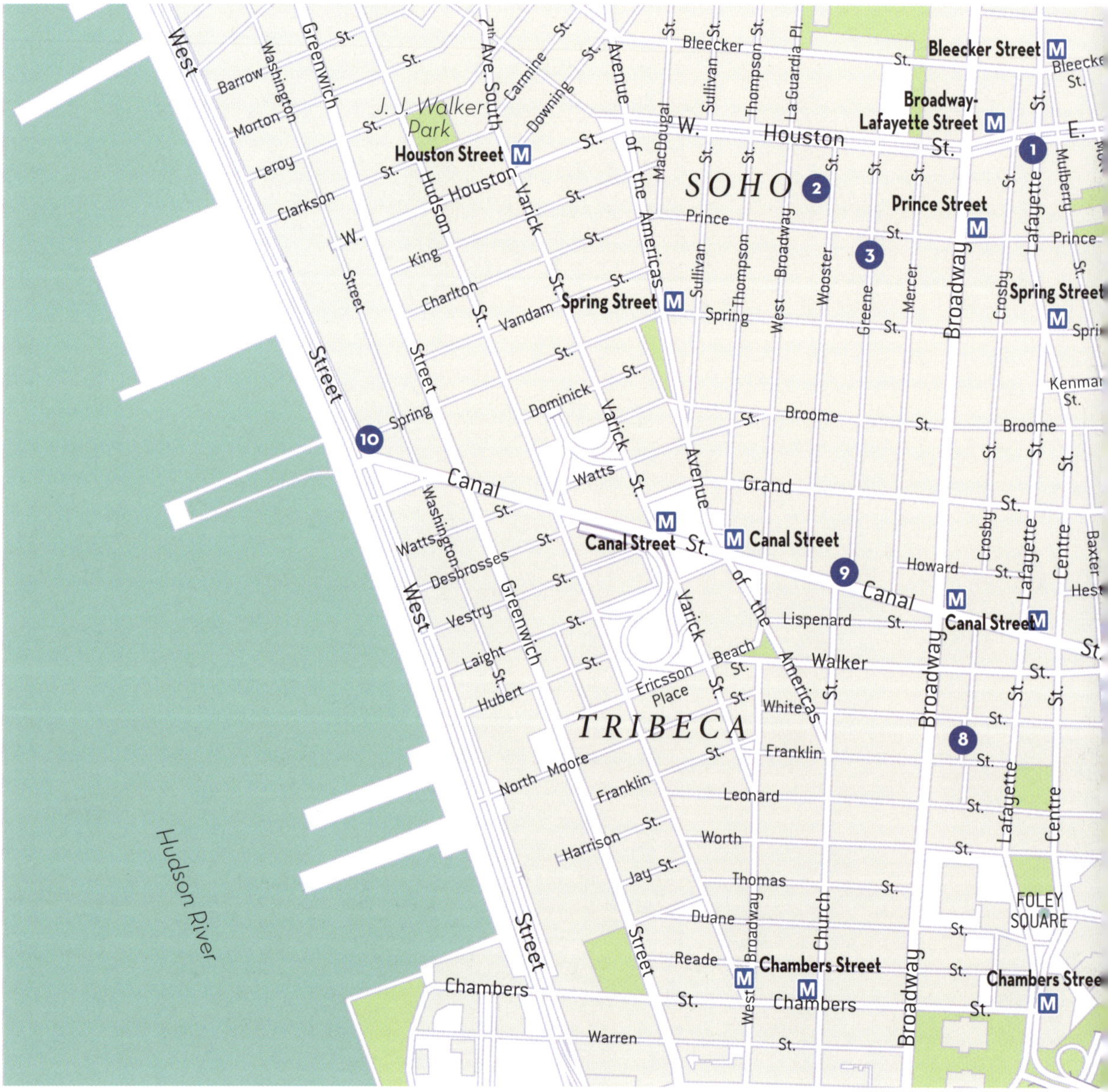

01. CROTON AQUEDUCT MANHOLE COVERS *p. 50*

02. *THE NEW YORK EARTH ROOM* *p. 52*

03. THE FLOATING MAP ON GREENE STREET *p. 54*

04. KEHILA KEDOSHA JANINA SYNAGOGUE *p. 56*

05. *HUA-MEI* BIRD MEN OF SARA D. ROOSEVELT PARK *p. 58*

06. THE SLAVE GALLERIES AT ST. AUGUSTINE'S *p. 60*

Lower East Side-
2 Avenue
Houston St.
E. Houston St.
Hamilton Fish Park
Chrystie
Forsyth
Eldridge
Allen
Orchard
Ludlow
Essex
Norfolk
Suffolk
Clinton
Attorney
Ridge
Pitt
Columbia
Stanton
Rivington
Sara D. Roosevelt Park
Bowery
Elizabeth
Delancey Street
Essex Street
Delancey St.
WILLIAMSBURG BRIDGE
North
South
Lewis
Broome
LITTLE ITALY
LOWER EAST SIDE
Grand
Mott
Hester
Seward Park
Canal St.
STRAUS SQUARE
East Broadway
Rutgers
Henry
Madison
Montgomery
Gouverneur St.
Water
South
Cherry
Bayard
CHINATOWN
Columbus Park
Worth
CHATHAM SQUARE
Division
Pike
MANHATTAN BRIDGE
Park Row
Pearl
Monroe
Franklin D. Roosevelt Drive
East River
N
0
200
400 m

01.

Photo 1: Fifth Avenue at 110th Street
4 and 6 trains/103rd Street
Photo 2: Jersey Street
B, D, F and M trains/Broadway – Lafayette

CROTON AQUEDUCT MANHOLE COVERS

Relics of a vast public water project

Two manhole covers, hidden in plain sight on Fifth Avenue and Jersey Street in SoHo, are nearly the only ones remaining in the city with the word "Croton" curving around the face. They're vestiges of the titanic engineering project that brought fresh water to Manhattan in the 1800s, and one cover (photo 2 opposite) is thought to be the city's oldest.

With rivers on three sides, you'd think that clean water wouldn't be a problem in Manhattan. In fact the rivers around the island are salty; two of them, the Harlem and East Rivers, aren't proper rivers at all but tidal straits. The springs and streams that supplied fresh water to the colonists gradually became polluted and were filled in, and most of the growing population came to rely on cisterns, wells, and rain barrels. Some of the effects of this you can guess: illness, disease, increased fire risk. Others not so much: alcoholism (liquor was cleaner than water) and the formation of the Chase Manhattan Bank, which began as a mostly phony water distribution service for the wealthy.

The Croton Aqueduct changed everything. Using technology that would make an ancient Roman yawn, the aqueduct relied on simple gravity to channel fresh water from the most suitable natural source, in this case the Croton River 40 miles to the north. Construction began in 1837, and just five years later 60 million gallons a day, descending at a rate of 15 vertical inches per mile, began flowing into Manhattan. There were two reservoirs in the city; the furthest south, the Croton Distributing Reservoir, was a magnificent aquatic fortress with granite walls 50 feet high and 25 feet thick. New Yorkers used to take promenades along the rim for an overlook of the entire city, and the beguiling sight of moonlight sparkling on the 4-acre lake within. The reservoir, built to echo the staid architecture of ancient Egypt, was intended to meet the city's water needs for centuries. It was overwhelmed in 50 years. A parallel system followed (still supplying Manhattan with 10% of its water today), but the enormous Croton Reservoir was razed for the construction of the main branch of the New York Public Library.

Traces of the aqueduct – paths, gatehouses, bridges – can be found throughout the Bronx and Manhattan.

1

2

02.

141 Wooster Street
diacenter.org
B, D, F and M trains/Broadway – Lafayette Street
N and R trains/Spring Street

THE NEW YORK EARTH ROOM

Three decades of just dirt

If the story of New York City is the story of real estate, then the *Earth Room* on Wooster Street is a tale of horror. In a second-floor loft of a Renaissance Revival building in one of the city's hottest areas lives ... a roomful of dirt. The dirt covers 3,600 square feet to a depth of 22 inches and weighs 280,000 pounds. According to commissioners Dia Art Foundation, *The New York Earth Room* is "an interior earth sculpture" – but mostly what it is is a roomful of dirt.

Cobbled Wooster Street is lined with shoe stores and boutiques; the only hint that number 141 houses a work by a major American artist is a plaque directing the visitor to ring bell 2B. As soon as you enter the narrow stair, you can sniff what's in store. "That's good," says William Dilworth behind the counter of the reception area. "I was afraid the smell had been fading over the years." Dilworth is the full-time curator of the sculpture. He has a mild smile and the contemplative air you might expect from a man who passes his days tending 140 tons of mute soil. "I water it, I turn it, I rake it." He also plucks out the green shoots that sprout from time to time, for this is real, living earth. It's dark and moist. There is nothing else in the large white space, and nothing between you and the earth but a knee-high glass barrier.

The work's creator, Walter De Maria (b. 1935) is a Minimalist and Land Artist perhaps best known for *Lightning Field*, an array of 400 stainless-steel poles planted upright in the New Mexican desert. Dilworth can answer any question about the nuts and bolts of the project, but leaves you to judge for yourself the mesmeric properties of dirt. The floor is sound: holes are dug to check. The earth goes all the way down. Where it came from is uncertain, but Dilworth's best guess is "somewhere in Pennsylvania." De Maria chose it for the color.

Dia Art Foundation pioneered the retooling of urban industrial spaces for art and has made a mission of funding site-specific installations like the *Earth Room*, on continuous exhibition at the present site since 1980. *The Broken Kilometer*, another Dia-commissioned work by De Maria, can be seen just two blocks away at 393 West Broadway. The work is composed of 500 polished 2-meter-long brass rods arranged on the floor.

FACE
141
STAND
PIPE

03.

110 Greene Street
N and R trains/Prince Street

THE FLOATING MAP ON GREENE STREET

Milling ants or electrons

There's an alien scrawl in the sidewalk of Greene Street that takes a moment to puzzle out. At first it would seem to be a blown-up flowchart or circuit board, and these guesses are close to the mark. The stainless-steel pattern is a work of urban art by Belgian artist and architect Françoise Schein, and has long held the title of New York City's largest subway map.

"My life as an artist began," says Schein in her project notes, "on a sidewalk in SoHo." The artist had come to New York in 1978 to study urban design at Columbia. Immersed in the literature of mathematics and the dawning information age, she became bewitched by the brute force of New York transit. "This subway fascinated me: its filth, its life, its graffiti, the millions of travelers who used it every day like milling ants or electrons in a computer ..." She had a creative flash flying into New York, watching from the jet window as the city's strings of lights approached: it was like plunging into an enormous microchip.

Schein would get the chance to translate these impressions into work when real-estate developer Tony Goldman asked her in 1984 what she would do with the sidewalk in front of his building on Greene Street. Schein proposed a project called *Subway Map Floating* on a New York Sidewalk; Goldman immediately answered: "I'm buying it."

Illustrating the New York tenet that no one ever got anywhere by being timid, Schein spent the next year presenting her map to a jury of the SoHo community board; she then had to endure the mocking eye of the Department of Transportation officer, who made the young architect in tee-shirt and tennis shoes return dozens of times to explain why New York needed a gigantic puzzle of urban philosophy underfoot. Once the map was approved, Schein got to work cutting and welding stainless steel, pouring terrazzo, blowing her own glass for the station roundels.

The finished project earned her the 1985 Award for Excellence in Design from Mayor Koch.

Schein went on to make a niche of urban art in subways, with works in Lisbon, Brussels, Berlin, Paris, and Stockholm.

04.

280 Broome Street
kkjsm.org
B and D trains/Grand Street
J train/Bowery
F train/Delancey

KEHILA KEDOSHA JANINA SYNAGOGUE

The only Romaniote synagogue in the Western Hemisphere

Of the hundreds of synagogues that used to fill the Lower East Side in the late 1800s and early 1900s, only five remain that still function as free-standing houses of worship. Of these one is rarer still: the Janina Synagogue on Broome Street. It's the only Romaniote synagogue in the Western Hemisphere.

If you don't know what a Romaniote Jew is, there are good reasons. A small group outside of the major factions in Judaism, the Ashkenazim (originally centered around Germany) and the Sephardim (Spain and Portugal), the Romaniotes settled in Greece, and have traditions that go back to Roman times. As a group they were sometimes marginalized even by other Jews and in predominantly Ashkenazi New York they were even scorned. "They tended to look down on this community," says Marcia Ikonomopoulos, the Janina Museum director. "How could you be Jewish if you don't speak Yiddish? Well, we were. And we're still here."

Janina can be contrasted with the neighborhood's most regal house of worship, the Eldridge Street Synagogue. Eldridge offers a sweeping story that touches literally millions. By contrast, Janina's appeal is fine-grained. It's small. It's humble, even a little dowdy ("They were decoratively challenged," says Ikonomopoulos.) The main hall is divided, as is customary, with women seated above and men below, but the room is narrow and filled with sunlight pouring through the central skylight. "If a man was sitting over here," says Ikonomopoulos, "his wife would be up there opposite, and they could look upon each other. He could tell her to be quiet if she was talking with her friends, she'd be able to tell him to stop reading the newspaper. I like to define this community as less-neurotically-Orthodox."

For Ikonomopoulos, this understatement is key. Even the synagogue's principal Torah has a utilitarian simplicity: the decorative crown on the olive-wood case is a simple brass cutout with a Star of David punched into it with what might have been a nail. "They weren't looking to impress anybody," she says. "They were looking for a place where they could feel at home."

The Greek Romaniotes are the longest continuous Jewish presence in the European Diaspora: over 2,300 years.

EXIT
EXIT

05.

Chrystie Street at Broome
nycgovparks.org/parks/saradroosevelt
F train/2nd Avenue
4 and 6 trains/Spring Street
J train/Bowery

HUA-MEI BIRD MEN OF SARA D. ROOSEVELT PARK

A corner of the park, a thousand years of tradition

In the dark and exciting 1980s, Sara Delano Roosevelt Park in Chinatown was a grey, trashy place, full of drug dealers and nodding junkies. Then, slowly, a group of pioneering Chinese immigrants began claiming a section of turf for their incongruous hobby: the breeding and showing of songbirds. Now on any given morning you can see the bird men smoking or chatting, leaning on the rails as they watch over dozens of exotic birds in carved bamboo cages. The practice goes back a thousand years.

The birding area is closed off by a rope, from which tiny songbirds hang in small cages. Behind, on cobbles, stand larger cages: these contain dark yellow birds just under a foot long with bright beaks and amazing eyes. "That's the hua-mei," says Tommy Chan. "It's the main attraction bird." The hua-mei is a thrush native to China, where its song evokes romance, something like the nightingale's does in the West. Chan is a breeder and collector. He wears his long black hair in a ponytail, topped by a fur cap, and silver rings on his fingers; the wisps of his graying beard are tied off with a rubber band. He's the man you'd naturally, and accurately, finger for top bird man. "In Ming Dynasty," he says, "the famous poets, they are using the eye of this bird to describe a pretty lady. They say: 'how pretty your eyes are, like *hua-mei*.'" (In Chinese *hua-mei* means "painted brow.") "And if you're a good singer they say: 'you can sing like a *hua-mei*.'"

If one hua-mei singing is poetry, twenty or so together sounds like it would be hell. But strangely, it's not. The birds are very active, dodging, twisting, the more energetic clawing backflips along the inside of the cage. Some even twist their heads sideways to press their remarkable circled eyes to the bars to get a better look at you while they trill, or thrust their open beaks through the gaps around the door. Each hua-mei has a distinct song. "This is different from most birds," says Chan. "If you hear your own bird for a while, when it sings, you know it's yours."

Asked if the bird he holds is one of his own, he blinks, and explains Rule Number One. "You never touch another man's bird."

06.

333 Madison Street
staugnyc.org
F train/East Broadway or Delancey Street
J, M and Z trains/Essex Street

THE SLAVE GALLERIES AT ST. AUGUSTINE'S

A pew for the hidden

St. Augustine's Church on Henry Street has pews on the ground floor, and a gallery overhead. In the back, above the upper seating on either side, there is yet another level tucked up behind a kind of open transom. These recessed spaces, original to the church's construction in 1828, have been called the slave galleries. They were designed to seat Black churchgoers with the idea of making them as difficult to notice as possible.

A visit of St. Augustine's begins with a historical outline of the building and the area; everyone sits in the relative comfort of the lower pews, sunlight angling through the lancet windows and fans humming from the corners. Then things take a sensory turn: visitors are invited to file up the cramped stair at the back to the separate galleries, sit on the bare wooden platform seats, and try to grasp the feelings of the people who were made to accept this concealment as their natural due. "Just close your eyes for a moment," says Reverend Hopper, the church deacon, "and imagine." On this visit, the temperature in the gallery is well over 100 degrees: the visitors are sweating through their clothes. The view down to the lower levels of the church is framed by the transom, with only half the pulpit visible, but the effect is more than visual. The open area down there feels like another, distant dimension.

Deacon Hopper has worked with the Lower East Side Tenement Museum to restore the galleries. Every board and nail has been preserved, and the western side has been painted, based on expert analysis, to match how it looked 180 years ago. The term "slave gallery" is culturally correct, but this one raises questions. New York abolished slavery on July 4, 1799, according to a system of "gradual emancipation:" males born before that date would remain slaves until the age of 28, and females until 25. St. Augustine's was constructed a year after the last male slave was freed, but the existence of the galleries demonstrates that freedom can lag behind emancipation.

07.

55 St. James Place
shearithisrael.org / 1654society.org
J and Z trains/Chambers Street
4, 5 and 6 trains/Brooklyn Bridge – City Hall

SHEARITH ISRAEL CEMETERY

America's other pilgrims

This simple plot is not only the oldest colonial landmark in Manhattan, it's the oldest Jewish cemetery anywhere in the United States.

The first Jewish New Yorker on record is Jacob Barsimson, who arrived from Holland on the ship *Pereboom* (Pear Tree) with a mission that would resonate through the city's – and the nation's – history: to find out whether a larger Jewish population would be welcome in New Amsterdam. The short answer was yes; the long answer reflects the familiar pattern of harassment. Governor Stuyvesant (see page 76) wanted no part of the "deceitful business" of Jewish settlers, and clergyman Johannes Megapolensis delivered a rant that will bring a grin to the face of anyone who revels in New York's incurable variety. "For as we have here Papists, Mennonites and Lutherans among the Dutch;" he wrote, "also many Puritans or Independents, and many atheists and various other servants of Baal among the English, it would create a still greater confusion, if the obstinate and immovable Jews came to settle here."

They came; they stayed. Two months after Barsimson the first group arrived from Recife (now in Brazil) following a sequence of trials that read like a historical thriller: escape from the Inquisition-crazed Portuguese, a desperate dash for Europe, capture by Spanish pirates, and finally rescue by a French privateer. A group of wealthy Jewish merchants and their families arrived from Holland in 1655; in the same year the Dutch West Indian Company granted the new community the right to "reside and traffic" in the city. You can judge from the record how eager these pioneering Jews were to have their own cemetery: the first petition for one was refused on the grounds that nobody had died yet.

The very first Shearith Israel Cemetery dates from 1656; its exact location is unknown, but it was likely very near or on Chatham Square, a stone's throw from the second cemetery we can see today. For a spot so charged with history, it seems willfully unromantic now: a handful of grave markers, half of them illegible, behind a fence.

Across the street is the Chinatown Martial Arts and Fitness Center; south are the baleful Chatham Green Apartments snaking along the square; north is a traffic cop on the corner of St. James Place and Oliver Street, wheeling her white gloves and shouting "Come on, pick it up! Pick it up people, let's *GO*!"

08.

Cortlandt Alley between Franklin and White Streets
mmuseumm.com
N, Q, R, J and 6 trains/Canal Street

MMUSEUMM

Exhibits in an abandoned freight elevator

Mmuseumm is an exhibition space, little more than 5 feet square, that occupies an abandoned freight elevator shaft in a downtown Manhattan alley. You can only enter on the weekend, but the steel doors come equipped with viewing ports and a number to call to learn about the odd objects that line the walls (all visible at once), making it the only 24-hour museum in the city. "Welcome," says Alex Kalman, springing the padlock on the doors and sweeping his arm with self-mocking grandeur. The first thing to say about the tiny space is: it walks a narrow line of what constitutes "museumness." Trim design, white molding, rich velvet, etched brass plaques. There's even a "café" (a narrow electric espresso machine) and a "gift shop" (a foot-wide shelf with pencils printed with the tasteful Mmuseumm logo). Because the trappings are so finely observed, it's a challenge to figure out whether you're in a parody or not. Kalman comes clean: "We're absolutely playing with the idea of a museum," he says. But it's thoughtful play. Kalman founded the space with his business partners and friends since high school as another outlet for the ideas the trio explores at Red Bucket Films (the offices are around the corner on Broadway). "We're saying: Why can't we call this a museum? But at the same time trying to really respect the key ingredients." All of this falls apart if the exhibits fail to intrigue, and that you'll decide for yourself. But expect objects with built-in riddles. Why is that plain brown shoe here? It's the one hurled at George W. Bush by an Iraqi reporter in 2008. Come also to see ornate soap carvings by gifted neo-Nazi zealots with eternities of free time in prison. Or probably the only collection of Disney-themed children's bulletproof backpacks. "No art for art's sake," says Kalman, stating a cardinal rule. "These have to be artifacts, things that have kind of passed through society as part of our nature. And it's up to us to look at society through them." Kalman, curious and good-humored, has created a testing ground for what we consider worth elevating. Mmuseumm isn't a comment on what an exhibition space should be, only on what it could be if he and his buddies ran it. Which, lucky for Cortlandt Alley, they do.

RAKO

09.

Greene Street at Canal Street
N and R trains/Canal Street

HOLLOW SIDEWALKS

A transparent sidewalk

On the east side of Greene Street where it starts at Canal, for decades there have hung notices alerting pedestrians and drivers to watch out for "hollow sidewalks." The handwritten signs are a little alarming, as though locals are in a fight with a menace that claws hungrily under the city crust. But hollow sidewalks are just a feature of the neighborhood architecture.

SoHo was once filled with genteel brick houses. The area began to fall out of favor with the city's wealthy in the mid-1800s when retail and wholesale businesses moved in and south of Houston gradually became a universal supply center: dry goods, glassware, fur, tobacco. A building type emerged to suit these forces, a kind of combination office, manufacturing and retail space. Builders split the difference between cheap and elegant through use of the hot new material, cast iron. A businessman would sit in his offices on the top floor while a hive of immigrant workers buzzed below, and at the same time on the street a colorful awning shaded tall display windows where the enterprise put its best face to the public. Below all this – below street level – is where hollow sidewalks come in.

Keep your eyes on the ground here and it won't be long before you notice a characteristic pattern: a metal lattice of hexagons with – where the whole thing isn't tarred or painted over – circlets of scarred glass. The technical term is "vault lights," and essentially what they are is a transparent sidewalk. The multi-use buildings include underground storage that extends all the way to the street; the circles of glass let the sunlight in. They're even cleverer than that: in some vault lights, the glass stem is angled at the bottom so light will be prismed into the basement's deeper and darker recesses.

One effect of vault lights is more fragile sidewalks; the notices are to keep heavy machinery off. It's not an empty precaution: sidewalks have caved in before. One of the uglier details of the 1911 fire at the Triangle Shirtwaist Factory – the third most lethal disaster in New York's history – was bodies falling from the burning building, and right through the ground to the basement. Another effect: Greene Street has no green. Hollow sidewalks are dirtless, and so treeless.

10.

336 Spring Street
1, 2, A, C and E trains to Canal Street

THE SPRING STREET SALT SHED

A house for salt

At Pier 34 on the west side, where the Holland Tunnel dives into Manhattan, passers-by have long wondered about the matching pairs of bare brick towers that rise several stories at the water's edge. They look important, but clearly weren't built for housing people: no balconies, few windows, no lights.

The towers (one pair visible in the background of the photo) are in fact ventilation shafts for the unseen tunnel, but their status as reigning enigmas was recently demolished. In 2015 this giant block of brute concrete, faceted like a crystal, rose at the same location. Both old and new are humble infrastructure – but how far we've come. The towers are of warm brick with subtle detailing to satisfy the elegance demanded by the 1920s. The new building looks like it fell from Planet X. What is it?

A place to store salt. Around 5,000 tons, or a small mountain. When snow and ice hit Manhattan, sanitation trucks – "salt spreaders" – stock up here on their rounds. The volume and jutting angles are inspired by the structure of salt itself. Here the concept of form following function is taken to a literally granular level; the salt shed is a blown-up crystal. The building follows a manifest logic, but its beauty seems detached from comfort and emotion. This is a house for salt. It's looking out for salt. It does what salt wants. The side facing the river is taller than the other, and the walls slope out. Yes, this decreases the footprint to leave more room for pedestrians, but the slope is precisely calculated from the angle that a mountain of salt assumes when the crystals naturally stack on one another in repose. Again, the tiny grain is the determining factor.

The work of Dattner Architects and WXY Architecture & Urban Planning, the salt shed has bewitched architecture fans and won numerous awards. Richard Dattner stresses the hidden power in the humble (the next time you don't skid into a pole, thank the Sanitation Department) and seems to be just getting used to the idea that his building has become an object of wonder. "It's a form that is so abstract," he says, "Everybody can read their own meaning. I love hearing different interpretations."

HOUSTON TO 14TH

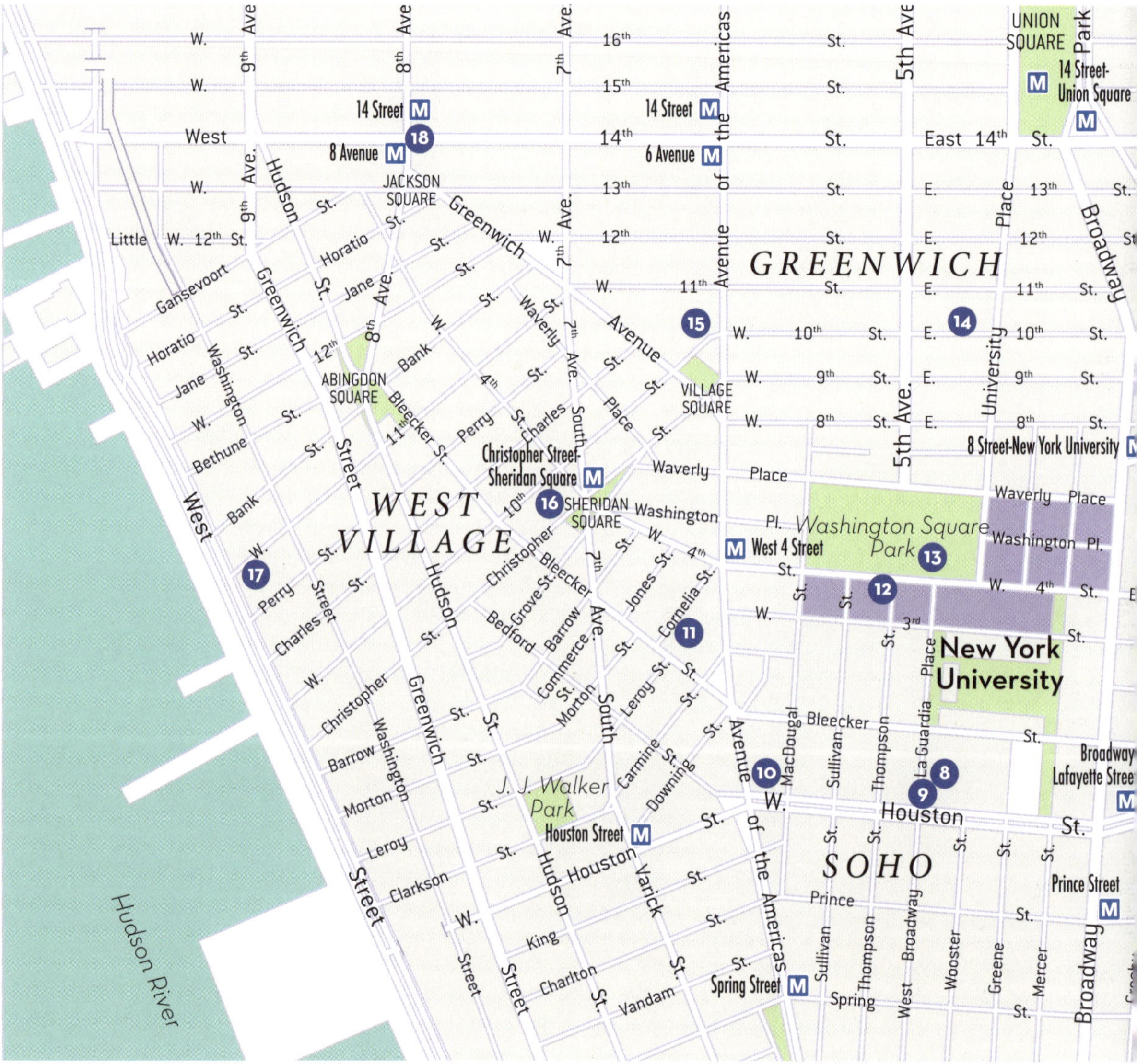

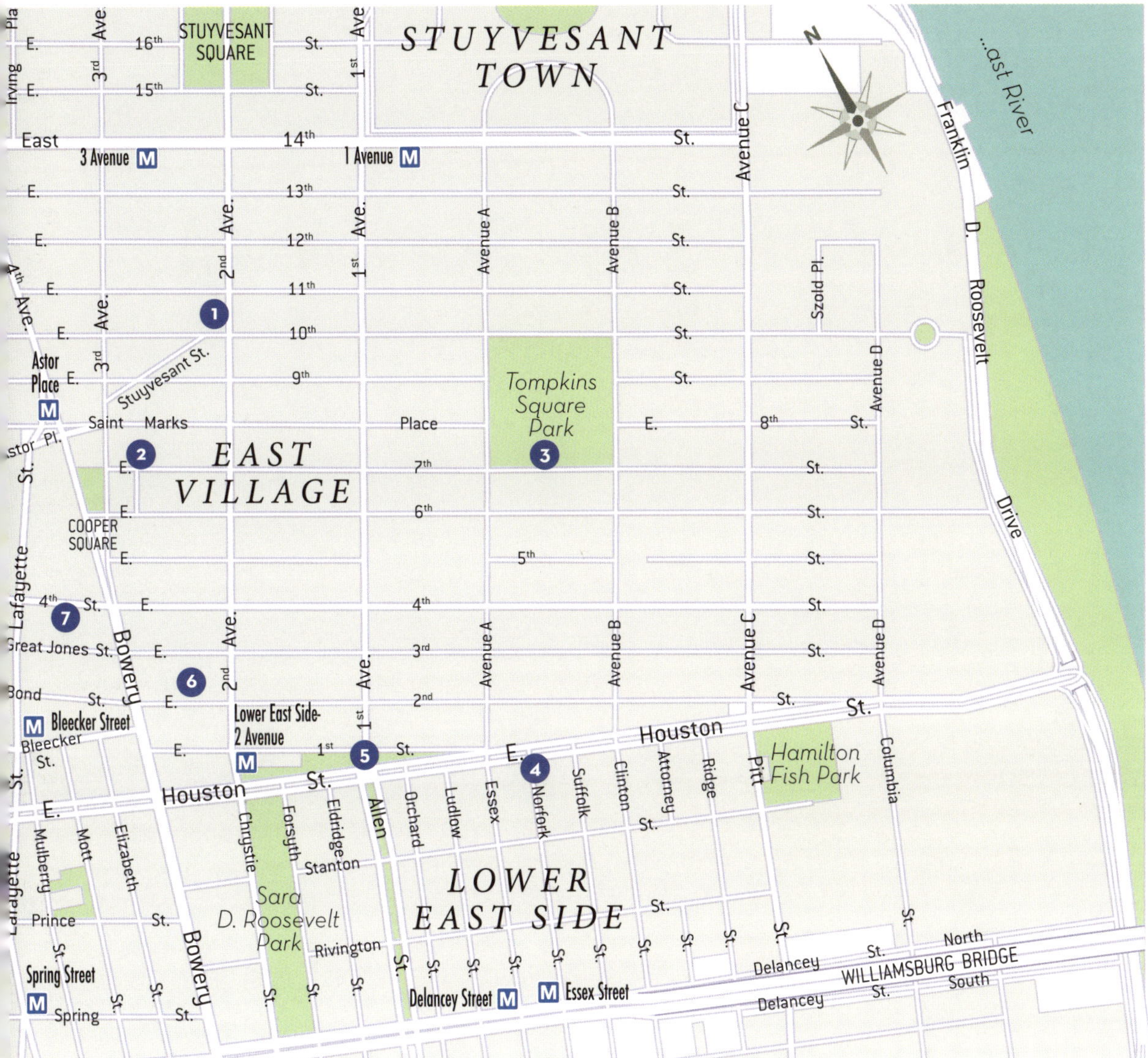
STUYVESANT TOWN
STUYVESANT SQUARE
EAST VILLAGE
LOWER EAST SIDE
COOPER SQUARE
Tompkins Square Park
Hamilton Fish Park
Sara D. Roosevelt Park
East River
Franklin D. Roosevelt Drive
WILLIAMSBURG BRIDGE
3 Avenue
1 Avenue
Astor Place
Bleecker Street
Lower East Side-2 Avenue
Spring Street
Delancey Street
Essex Street
Saint Marks Place
Stuyvesant St.
Houston St.
Bowery
Lafayette St.
Great Jones St.
Bond St.
Avenue A
Avenue B
Avenue C
Avenue D
Szold Pl.
Columbia St.
Pitt St.
Ridge St.
Attorney St.
Clinton St.
Suffolk St.
Norfolk St.
Essex St.
Ludlow St.
Orchard St.
Allen St.
Eldridge St.
Forsyth St.
Chrystie St.
Elizabeth St.
Mott St.
Mulberry St.
Prince St.
Spring St.
Stanton St.
Rivington St.
Delancey St.
1
2
3
4
5
6
7

01.

St. Mark's Church-in-the-Bowery
131 East 10th Street
stmarksbowery.org
4 and 6 trains/Astor Place
L train/3rd Avenue

A.T. STEWART'S BROKEN VAULT

His body was stolen

At St. Mark's Church in-the-Bowery there are flat stones arrayed in the ground: the covers of burial vaults. One of these lies in a privileged spot near the center of the East Side, but it's a shambles: there's no inscription and the stone is broken to pieces. On the map distributed by the church this plot is marked 9D, Alexander T. Stewart, with the titillating note: *His body was stolen*.

Dubbed the "inventor of the department store," A.T. Stewart was one of those charmed and driven New Yorkers who manage to strangle every advantage the city offers. The Belfast immigrant made his fortune in textiles; when he turned to luxury shopping he built a marble palace near City Hall that was so lovely the *Herald* wrote: "We hope Mr. Stewart doesn't mean to disfigure his beautiful edifice sacred to the mysteries of Dry Goods with a sign." Stewart didn't need a sign.

That store was followed by an even more spectacular iron and glass emporium further uptown, and when he was buried in St. Mark's in 1876, Stewart's fortune was judged at $40 million – the equivalent of about $800 million today.

On a November night in 1878, Stewart's crypt was broken into, and his remains hauled out. It wasn't easy: the deft robbers had to get past the stone, unscrew a cedar chest, cut through a lead box, break a copper coffin, and stuff the dusty old millionaire in a sack – and all without waking the neighbors. There were no suspects.

When the bodysnatchers came forward (through a lawyer) they demanded $250,000 for the remains. During the next two years the executor haggled while Stewart's wife had ghoulish nightmares. Finally a relative of the widow met three masked men on a lonely country road in Westchester and traded $20,000 for a gunnysack. Inside were human bones and a piece of cloth lining from Stewart's casket. The bones – never proven to be Stewart's – now rest on Long Island.

You can still see Stewart's Marble Palace filling the entire block of Broadway between Reade and Chambers Streets. Five stories of Italianate elegance, it was America's first commercial establishment with a lavish exterior. Note the bronze clock bolted to the corner, a relic of the Sun (the newspaper's genial slogan "It shines for all" appears below the dial) which bought the palace in 1917. It's now known as the Sun Building.

02.

McSorley's Old Ale House
15 East 7th Street
mcsorleysoldalehouse.nyc
6 train/Astor Place
N and R trains/8th St – NYU

THE REWARD POSTER FOR THE CAPTURE OF JOHN WILKES BOOTH

$100,000 reward

According to legend, nothing has been removed from the walls of McSorley's Old Ale House since 1910, when founder John McSorley died. It's an easy legend to believe. The bar, New York's oldest, is heaped with an attic's worth of beautiful junk. Even the dust is respected. "The health department made us clean them off last year," says the young lady behind the bar; she's nodding at an old gaslight fixture – the same one you can see in John Sloan paintings of the bar from the early 1900s – decorated with wishbones. Over her shoulder on the wall is a yellowed poster, a broadside of the sort that hasn't been used in a hundred years.

"$100,000 REWARD," it reads, "THE MURDERER of our late beloved President, Abraham Lincoln, IS STILL AT LARGE." The date at the top: April 20, 1865, five days after the president was killed.

Broadside and alehouse both strengthen a remarkable connection between Lincoln and New York City. Rural simplicity was central to the president's appeal, but he didn't become a contender until this quality was thrown into relief in America's biggest and dirtiest city. In late February of 1860, a beardless Lincoln stood before a crowd at Cooper Union and delivered a soaring speech that would fix his destiny. "No man ever before," reported the New-York Tribune, "made such an impression on his first appeal to a New York audience." Afterward Cooper Union founder Peter Cooper escorted Lincoln across the street to the bar, then only a few years old. The chair Lincoln used, cemented in a pile of cobwebbed miscellany, is now also part of the permanent decor.

Five years after Lincoln raised a glass here, he was shot by John Wilkes Booth. Secretary of War Edwin Stanton relayed descriptions of the assassin and his accomplices, as well as the unprecedented reward, starting a breathless manhunt that lasted ten days. Is the McSorley's broadside authentic? It doesn't matter: the bar has character to burn.

The poster is slightly different from other versions you'll see, but several were issued, and the text, spelling errors and all, exactly repeats the War Secretary's telegram. There's a broadside in the Ohio Historical Society that is so identical to the one in McSorley's it's fishy: even the wrinkles and ink smudges match. But if one is a copy, which one? At a bar that drinks this deeply from history, it's a fair question.

War Department Washington, April 20, 1865,
$100,000 REWARD
THE MURDERER
Of our late beloved President, Abraham Lincoln,
IS STILL AT LARGE.
$50,000 REWARD
$25,000 REWARD
$25,000 REWARD
WHAT - ME WORRY?

03.

Tompkins Square Park
L train/1st Avenue

THE HARE KRISHNA TREE

Where the sect began

The Hare Krishna movement is based on 5,000-year-old Hindu scripture, but it started in the East Village. The founder, Srila Prabhupada (born Abhay Charan De in Calcutta), a scholar and translator of Vedanta texts, arrived in New York in 1965 as many do: with little money and big ideas. He rented a storefront at 26 Second Avenue and, relying mostly on charisma, immediately began gathering disciples for his spiritual revolution. The movement was incorporated in the summer of 1966 under the name International Society for Krishna Consciousness, and so a mystical tradition of "Would you like to buy some of our literature?" was born.

The American elm tree in Tompkins Square Park, already venerable in its own way (the elms here date back to the park's official founding in 1873), was the backdrop of the defining event of the Hare Krishna movement. On October 9, 1966, Swami Prabhupada, encircled by followers, led a collective chant of the Krishna mantra for the first time outside India. The mantra, of great antiquity, goes: *Hare Krishna, Hare Krishna, Krishna Krishna, Hare Hare, Hare Rama, Hare Rama, Rama Rama, Hare Hare.* Prabhupada called it "The sound representation of the Supreme Lord." The swami died in 1977, but the shop front on Second Avenue, now the Hare Krishna Temple, is still there.

OTHER NOTABLE TREES IN NEW YORK

New York City has several notable trees.
An English elm in Washington Square Park nicknamed "The Hanging Tree" due to an (unfounded) reputation as a site of execution, was planted in 1770 – the oldest living thing in Manhattan. In 1936, on the centennial of the opening of Madison Avenue, a tree from former president James Madison's estate in Virginia was planted on the east side of Madison Square Park and lives there still. For years a legend has persisted (often in the mouths of Conservancy guides themselves) that a mulberry tree in the Shakespeare Garden of Central Park was a graft from one planted in Stratford-on-Avon by the Bard himself. Not only did the tree blow down in 2006, analysis determined that the Shakespeare business was balderdash. The pear tree that Peter Stuyvesant brought from Holland in 1647 stood on the corner of 13th Street and Third Avenue for 200 years before it was knocked down in a horse cart smash-up. A replacement pear tree, and a plaque, mark the spot now.

04.

178 Norfolk Street
F train/2nd Avenue

LENIN ON NORFOLK STREET

Communism, New York style

The bronze statue of Lenin, 18 feet tall, arm raised to salute the Workers of the World, used to crown the roof of a luxury apartment building on Houston Street. The father of communism faced south, and as you gazed up at him, it was hard to overlook that within the scope of that confident salute teems the original hive of unchecked Kapital, Wall Street. In fact, a New York monument to Lenin pointing any direction but upside down is hard to reconcile. The statue, then, is some kind of joke.
Not quite. Lenin is a later addition to the building, which was constructed in 1988 when Houston Street fell on the fault line between gentrifying East Village and a much poorer Lower East Side. The 70s were hard on Black and Puerto Rican communities here; with a hot real estate market in the 80s, the money marched in and the streets became a class war battleground. M&CO, the design firm that created the building's "identity," thought the name should have a touch of dread to attract those magical New York animals, "people with resources who wanted to live in a hip, extreme and even dangerous neighborhood." The name they settled on: Red Square. The Lenin statue, then, is nothing more than marketing savvy.
Not quite. The developer of Red Square, Michael Rosen, was once an NYU professor of radical sociology with a course called "Power and Politics." A guy like that knows from Lenin. Also, Rosen's post-Red Square activity – subsidized housing for the poor, people with AIDS victims of domestic violence – is not the résumé of a cynic. The 18-foot statue, then, is more like the icing on a luxury apartment publicity stunt by a developer with an eye on a longer goal of social responsibility.
But where did it come from? In 1994, an associate of Rosen's found Lenin in the backyard of a *dacha* near Moscow. Originally commissioned by the Soviet state, it was hardly finished when communism went south. When you already have a quirky luxury building in Manhattan called Red Square, you snap your fingers at the shipping costs.

In 2016 the statue was moved just across from the Red Square to the roof of 178 Norfolk Street.

05.

Corner of First Avenue and East 1st Street
F train/2nd Avenue

ROOF HOUSES

A home in the air

There are top dwellers in the city who take the idea of a penthouse a step further and actually build a house – that is, a nice little house like one you'd expect to see on the ground – on a roof. It's like a patch of suburbia in the shadow of a water tower. The highest are undetectable from the street, but you can see two low ones within walking distance of each other in the East Village, and one on a ten-story building on the Upper West Side.

The first, on the corner of East 13th Street and Third Avenue, is perched atop a famous address: the original home of Kiehl's apothecary ("Since 1851") and the site of Peter Stuyvesant's pear tree (see page 76). The elevated home, with its chimney and windows and clapboard siding, is a fake: according to Time Out, the "house" contains not an eccentric family, but only boiler rooms and roof-access stairwells.

The second (pictured) looks like it was lifted in a tornado from a whaling village up north and dropped on the corner of First Avenue and East 1st Street. Shingle siding, crawling ivy, an octagonal pilot house with a weathervane on top: it has the hallmarks of habitation. All that's missing is a bearded man in oilskin flaking scrimshaw on the taxis below. Whether or not the little house is currently tenanted is uncertain.

The third roof house is further uptown, on the top of 210 West 78th Street (best seen from Broadway and 77th). There's no doubt this one was built as a dwelling: in 1997 the Times interviewed the builder/dweller. Andrew Tesoro converted a tiny 400-square-foot penthouse into a three-story "ski chalet" with a copper roof pitched 60 degrees. His front porch drops ten floors straight down. "I love the view," Tesoro said, "because you feel like you're kind of on top, but you also feel like you're embraced by all of it."

ROOF LIFE

The Ansonia residence at 2109 Broadway used to have a farm on the roof, with a "small bear" available for parties. The Pan Am Building's helicopter service (midtown to JFK in 7 minutes) ran in 1977 until an accident killed five people. Both best and worst rooftop idea: the Empire State Building pinnacle was originally designed to serve as a zeppelin dock. A landing was only attempted once: no one had figured on the stiff winds.

BUS LANES PHOTO ENFORCED
SPEED LIMIT 30
E 1 ST
ONE WAY
ONE WAY
HOSPITAL
LA LINEA

06.

41 ½ 2nd Avenue
marblecemetery.org
4 and 6 trains/Bleecker Street
F train/2nd Avenue

NEW YORK MARBLE CEMETERY

A realm between realms

Two obscure cemeteries can be found only a couple of blocks from each other in the East Village. One is generally overlooked – the other might as well not exist. If you don't live next door or habitually pore over the city map, you'll be surprised to learn that in the middle of a block on Second Avenue you can walk through an iron gate, down a narrow passage, and emerge in a half-acre of emerald quad surrounded by old brick walls. Even the address, 41 ½, suggests that the spot is a realm between realms.

The New York Marble Cemetery, incorporated in 1831, is the oldest non-sectarian burial ground in New York. The nearby and similarly named New York City Marble Cemetery on 2nd Street was founded later the same year. "It's totally confusing," admits Caroline DuBois, NYMC president. She parses the difference between the two. "We haven't had a burial here in 75 years. The other one has had one every single year. They're twice as large, twice as many families, and you can see them all. They haven't disappeared from memory. We really disappeared." She means not only disappeared from the map: she means you can't see a single gravestone.

All of the bodies – a little over 2,000 – are in underground marble vaults. Six columns in 26 rows, 10 feet deep, but with roofs just inches under the grass. The cemetery's lawn is interrupted only by shrubs and trees; the names of the dead appear on plaques embedded in the brick walls. You'll find a former mayor of New York City, founders of New York University, and names associated with the city or written into the map: Varick, Scribner, Olmsted.

Today the cemetery can be visited, but only once a month, usually the fourth Sunday, and only during the summer. It's worth having to wait for a chance to stroll for a few minutes in this secret patch, which has been narrowly saved from a kind of double oblivion. "You should have seen it ten years ago," DuBois says, rolling her eyes. "It was a vacant lot full of dead cats." She rotates in place, pointing out the neighboring buildings: "This is a homeless shelter. That's a methadone clinic. That's a hotel. They come in at night through a hole that they punched through our wall. Used to be, when I came in to do any kind of event, the first thing I'd do is pick up the hypodermic needles and the whiskey bottles and the underpants."

07.

29 East 4th Street
merchantshouse.org
4 and 6 trains/Bleecker Street or Astor Place

MERCHANT'S HOUSE AND THE GHOST OF GERTRUDE TREDWELL

This damn stove was *moving* that day. You think I'm joking?

The thing about the Merchant's House is, it's haunted. The ladies in the office pretend to be coy about it, and the visiting high school kids pretend to be freaked out about it, and the very walls seem to suffer from performance anxiety.

There's a booklet available in the office that describes what to expect if you're lucky enough to piss the ghost off: blasts of frigid air, disembodied footsteps, rattling chinaware. You might catch a whiff of violet toilet water or toasted bread. When the ghost's presence is visible, it manifests as a swinging chandelier, or floating orbs of light, or – the jackpot – a tiny old woman in a floral hoop dress with a stormy look in her eyes that says: *Get out.*

The creepy old woman is Gertrude Tredwell, and her connection to this place is so personal, so organic, as long as the house stands the ghost stories will go with it. The youngest child of a wealthy importer, Gertrude was born in a canopy bed in the front bedroom on the second floor and lived in the house her entire life. As the rest of the family died off and New York society migrated north, she became increasingly isolated. At the end she rarely opened the front door, stuffed the windows with newspaper to keep out the drafts, and let the furniture turn slowly pale with dust. Just shy of 93 years old, she died in 1933 – in the front bedroom, lying in the very same bed she was born in.

Construction of the building dates from the distant period when washing water was drawn from a nearby well; thanks to Gertrude's uninterrupted tenancy, today the Merchant's House is a historical bonanza. Everything here – furniture, carpets, draperies, glass, china, clothing – is original. The only changes made after the old woman's death were electrical wiring and plumbing, and the addition of a castiron stove in the kitchen.

This foreign stove is one of the things that pisses Gertrude off. Clarice, a Jamaican woman who has been caretaker here for 20 years, tells the story: "I was down alone in the kitchen, and the stove started to move. I got scared, and I run up the step here and waited outside for 40 minutes in my smock and slippers! This damn stove was moving that day. You think I'm joking?"

08.

Silver Towers/University Village
Between Bleecker and West Houston Streets at LaGuardia Place
B, D, F and M trains/Broadway – Lafayette Street
4 and 6 trains/Bleecker Street

"SYLVETTE"

Monumental Picasso

Large-scale Picasso sculpture is a small category. America's first was erected in Chicago's Daley Plaza; at 50 feet tall, it's not often missed. The second was dedicated only a year later in 1968 but concealed in the Village, at the center of three humorless 30-story residential towers.

In truth it's only *almost* a Picasso: the master oversaw the project, but the concept and execution are the work of Norse artist Carl Nesjar. "I'm like the conductor of an orchestra," Nesjar said. "The composer gives me a piece of music and then it's up to me to see what I can do with it." Nesjar kept Picasso connected through drawings, photos, and samples of concrete. Cast first in black Norwegian basalt, the angular block was then coated in light-colored cement and sandblasted by Nesjar to create dark, permanent lines. The 30-ton sculpture rests on a hidden cement base ("Picasso doesn't like pedestals") to keep it from sinking into the underground parking garage directly beneath.

Picasso's trademark games of perspective are on display. The sculpture is a plane of two dimensions folded to create three, but is best experienced in four: the double-sided portrait invites you to circle around it, and as you do the woman's features change with the shifting vantage, creating a new portrait at every step. The original sculpture copied here was just a little over 2 feet tall; Picasso folded it from paper, then a sturdier version was cut from sheet metal and painted. Entitled "Sylvette", the subject is Sylvette David, Picasso's muse during 1954. David was only 17 when Picasso first saw her; the smitten artist convinced her to pose as a model when he gave her a portrait drawn from memory. Later a painter in her own right, David is thought to have started the vogue, through Picasso's adoring portraits, of the high ponytail later worn by Brigitte Bardot.

Nesjar's 36-foot-tall "Sylvette" is hemmed in and shadowed by the buildings around it, which house NYU faculty and graduate students. On a warm afternoon the young son of residents warily eyes a group of rowdy kids on the lawn. When his mother asks him if the kids are "too big" to play with, he shrugs her off and spends the next 15 minutes alone, ringing a soccer ball from Sylvette's monumental face.

09.

Corner of West Houston and LaGuardia Place
B, D, F and M trains/Broadway – Lafayette Street
4 and 6 trains/Bleecker Street
A, C and E trains/Spring Street

"TIME LANDSCAPE"

A living recreation of past Manhattan

There are three places in the city that specialize in getting the visitor closer to the vanished landscapes of New York before Europeans. One is wild (the primeval forest of the New York Botanical Garden, page 362); one is well-preserved (Inwood Hill Park, page 344); the third is artificial. "Time Landscape" on LaGuardia Place is part garden, part public art project. You might mistake the fenced trees for another of the several small decorative parks in the Village, but this spot has a hook: the plants within have been carefully selected as representatives of the Manhattan of half a millennium ago. It's a haven for the imagined past. As such, one of the goals is keeping you out: there are no benches, and no gates.

Bronx-born artist and designer Alan Sonfist conceived the project in 1965, very early days for the Land Art movement of the 60s and 70s. In his plan to create a patch of accurate ecology in the middle of the most man-made city on Earth, the first phase involved researching the botany and geology of untouched Manhattan marshland – the proto-Greenwich Village of sandy hills and streams, the one known to Lenape Indians. Sonfist then marshaled local residents to plant the wild grass, shrubs, flowers, and trees, evoking, according to the stated mission, "the hidden narrative of the Earth." The idea was to establish a foothold for a living recreation of the past: among the trees planted in 1978 were beech saplings that are today fully grown; the groundcover of wildflowers, aster and milkweed continues to flourish beneath them.

"Time Landscape" is too small for the visitor to project a wider Manhattan of virgin nature. It's an 80 by 40 foot rectangle that keeps to itself, crowded by asphalt, architecture, and constant ruckus. The work is like a zoo for plants: the trees grow in their artificial habitat, looking out on an environment they have no organic connection with. The visitor will be struck by an irony: recreating everything like it was took a lot of special work. If the "Time Landscape" has a point, this is it, and the pains taken to create and maintain it underline how completely that unspoiled landscape has been buried.

The Lenape Indians called Greenwich Village Sapokanikan, "tobacco fields," either because they grew tobacco here or saw the early Dutch do it.

10.

6th Avenue from Canal to Washington Place
Several options, a good starting point is A, C and E trains to Spring Street

THE MEDALLIONS OF THE AVENUE OF THE AMERICAS

An avenue for a hemisphere

You might have had this experience: you're waiting on the corner to cross Sixth Avenue and you look up to see that, for some reason, the country seal of Honduras hangs over your head. Or the seal of Cuba. Or Venezuela, or Grenada, or Dominica. Or even Canada, which seems frankly out of place. These medallions, bolted onto light posts, mark the whole lower part of the avenue. If you're still puzzled, know that you're not really on Sixth Avenue at all. Officially, you're on the Avenue of the Americas. In fact, for decades after it was named such in the 1940s, the words "Sixth Avenue" didn't appear on signs at all, until finally the Department of Transportation threw in the towel and put up both versions. The country medallions didn't help the idea of an Avenue of the Americas take hold. Here's the story:

"It was good, old, Sixth Avenue ever since that memorable day in 1811 when the city fathers changed the name from West Road." So begins a 1945 Times article. The tone is a little bitter – opposition to an Avenue of the Americas was widespread. The new name was confusing, awkward, and expensive – 1,700 subway cars would have to be remarked, for example – as well as an insult to the nations involved because so many of the buildings on Sixth Avenue were "eyesores."

Mayor Fiorello La Guardia, who signed the bill to make the change, left no room for argument, asserting that the idea had general approval ... "in this city, in this country, and in the entire hemisphere." What was the purpose? In short: business. The U.S. had goods to sell to Canada and Latin America, and recognized the need to be a buyer in return.

It was thought that if the name came first, the trade would follow. In addition to consulates along the avenue, the Sixth Avenue Association envisaged a sort of open market for the entire hemisphere, with buildings "physically and psychologically designed for this purpose."

The medallions went up with the new aluminum lampposts in the 1950s.

JAMAICA
TURKS AND CAICOS
WRONG WAY
NEW YORK
PUBLIC LIBRARY

11.

323 6th Avenue
A, B, C, D, E and M trains: West 4th Street
1 train: Christopher Street

IFC CENTER'S PEEPHOLES

Spyholes hidden in plain sight, redefining a sneak peak of a film

On Greenwich Village's particularly New York corner of West 3rd and 6th Avenue, pedestrians can expect to watch a basketball game, a person eating a Papaya Dog and a street fight – but few realize they can also watch a picture free of charge. Though millions pass it annually, the peepholes on the side of art house movie theater IFC Center remain a well-kept secret hidden in plain sight.

To find them, face the cinema's entrance and walk to the right; next, carefully scan the space between posters for two metal circles, set within a larger metal circle, about five feet off the ground. Now, slide up the tops of the smaller circles and take a peek into them: You're watching what's playing in theater five. "It's something that we've never drawn attention to," the cinema's current general manager, Harris Dew, said of the structural delights. "It's just something that people discover or they don't."

The architectural Easter eggs are the creation of the cinema's designer, the late Larry Bogdanow, who had "a playful sense of humor and thought it would be a fun sort of secret surprise for people to stumble upon occasionally" Dew explained. They were built in 2009, when what was previously a ground-floor cafe was converted into two additional theaters for IFC, which Bogdanow designed in the hull of the old Waverly Theater when it closed after six decades in business back in 2001.

"The Waverly was a mess of a theater," Bogdanow said in a 2005 interview shortly after renovations finished and the tastefully designed IFC at last opened in the Waverly's place. Where the Waverly, once a respected cinema, fell from grace in its final years, IFC offered a carefully curated selection of art films on seats imported from France, elevated popcorn options and such endearing built-in quirks as the peepholes.

IFC has since become a New York institution in its own right, and the peepholes an enduring secret – like clockwork, every few years, there's another set of social media users who post videos and images of them, having just found out about their charming existence. "We do see these, sort of, waves of people, finding out about it," said Dew, adding that every time someone new discovers them "they think that they're the first person to ever realize it. But, you know, we don't disabuse people of that notion."

Club Zero
Femme
The People's Joker
IFC
JULIETTE BINOCHE

12.

55 Washington Square South
judson.org
A, C, E, B, D, F and M trains/West 4th Street
N and R trains/8th Street – NYU

"ANGEL IN ADORATION" AT JUDSON MEMORIAL CHURCH

The artist's mistress

The Judson Memorial Church offers a superior collection of stained glass by painter and decorator John LaFarge: 15-foot lancet windows depicting evangelists, saints and other religious figures in the artist's innovative "opalescent glass" style. One side window, an isolated tondo only 35 inches across, provides a view into LaFarge's private life. Called "Angel in Adoration", the lovely figure there – wings, halo, hands crossed over her heart – has the face of Mary Whitney, LaFarge's mistress.

The artist and his mistress: LaFarge didn't invent it. You don't even have to go outside of Judson Memorial Church to strike on the theme: Augustus Saint-Gaudens, who drew the marble relief of the baptistery, took his sculpture models to bed, and Stanford White, one of the church's architects, was so fond of vulnerable young girls he's remembered by history as a kind of priapic demon. In fact if LaFarge stands out it's not for casual romance, but caring too much. When Whitney joined his atelier in 1880, the artist lost his head. "He was definitely goofy about her," says consultant Julie Sloan, overseer of the Judson Memorial stained-glass restoration in the 1990s. "He didn't go to Stanford White's girlie parties, he didn't have a lot of women on the side. His relationship with Whitney seems to be unique."

The two were lovers by 1892; LaFarge became increasingly estranged from his wife, with whom he had seven children. At the same time, Whitney's face starts appearing on LaFarge's angels. James Yarnall, the foremost LaFarge scholar, called the irony of using a mistress as the model for angels "colossal." In one image the artist even painted Whitney's face on a figure representing Chastity.

LaFarge was respected as an artist and art historian, but poor judgment largely defined his life. He destroyed his professional relationship with Louis Comfort Tiffany, colleagues took him to court for grand larceny, his own children refused to work for him, and he died with $13 in the bank. "He lacked the business sense," his son, who lacked the redundancy sense, later said.

For the largest display of Mary Whitney-inspired faces and figures, see LaFarge's mural at the Church of the Ascension on 10th Street. "She's most of the angels," says Julie Sloan.

13.

Around Washington Square Park
Steve Duncan's site: undercity.org
A, B, C, D, E, F and M trains/W 4 Street
N and R trains/8 Street – NYU

TRACKING MINETTA BROOK

An underground river flows through the Village

One of the most suggestive, eerie, and seemingly fictitious features of the Village is Minetta Brook, a river that flows secretly underground. There are tales of flooded restaurants, and men with fishing poles gathered around holes in the concrete floors of basements, and garden fountains tapping the black water deep below. But Minetta exists. It was once a creek full of trout; sometime in the early 1800s it got entombed by a blanket of humming metropolis.

Today you can follow the course of the buried stream as it flows from about Fifth Avenue and out to the Hudson River. With an ordinary flashlight you can even see it, but you'll need the tour plan of Steve Duncan, Internet personage and expert on all things subterranean.

"From the tops of bridges to the depths of sewer tunnels," according to Duncan, "these explorations of the urban environment help me puzzle together the interconnected, multidimensional history and complexity of the great metropolises of the world." The hidden stream is the subject of his doctoral thesis. It's also very clearly his obsession: when he talks about it – gesturing with scuffed hands, a rolled cigarette wagging from his lip – you know you've found an authority.

Here are the highlights of his recent tour of the Village's own hidden river:

- 45 West 12th Street: This house is a relic of the old stream course. It overlaps its neighbor oddly, and actually has a wedge-shaped floor plan. The creek used to cut a diagonal across the lot, and the structure was built to skirt it.
- 60 West 9th Street: The address doesn't interest us: what does is the manhole cover in the street out front. It's a DPW (Department of Public Works) type, with large holes. Look in one hole and shine a flashlight down another. The water you see, according to Duncan, is a combination of "natural water flow and water used by residents in the area." Minetta, in other words, has been channeled into the city's infrastructure.
- Minetta Street: Here, as the name indicates, is deep in Brook territory. The kinked shape of this street (unique in Manhattan) is said to follow the path of the old water. If you hunt out the manhole cover – a DPW "hexagon" model like the one above – you'll see a steady flow, and be as close to the original stream as you can get without a crowbar and hip waders.

14.

7 East 10th Street
nycgovparks.org/parks/washingtonsquarepark
L, 4, 5 and 6 trains/Union Square – 14th Street
N and R trains/8th Street – NYU

DE FOREST HOUSE

Unique in New York

Even those who generally resent the word "picturesque" will allow that 10th Street in Greenwich Village has the quality, and lots of it. Variety, too. The authoritative *American Institute of Architects Guide to New York (AIA)* assigns half a dozen influences to the street: Neoclassical, Italianate, Gothic Revival, Venetian Gothic, Bavarian, Victorian. But this is just a warm-up for the alien excesses of the five-story house just east of Fifth Avenue. "Unique in New York," reads the AIA, "is the exotic, unpainted, and intricately carved teakwood bay window which adorns No. 7."

"Unique" is not easy to pull off in this town. If you're familiar with East Indian architecture, you'll know what you're looking at; if not, the house might as well have dropped from space. The balcony is made entirely of wood, and every surface is carved in delicate filigree. The decoration starts at the front door and swarms all over the jutting oriel, and continues further up, and even spreads as if through some animating charm to the adjacent building: vines and leaves and scales; moons, birds, elephants, flowers.

Lockwood de Forest, the man behind this marvel, was one of the founders of the prominent decorative arts firm Associated Artists. His interest in East Indian carving was professional and personal. After a wedding trip to the subcontinent in 1873, the designer was so impressed with the arresting style, he set up a woodworking facility at Ahmedabad to create hand-carved pieces for the export market. In 1887, after buying Nos. 7 and 9 on 10th Street, he ordered simple brick architecture and outfitted it with this one-of-a-kind adornment. The building has since been divided into separate units, but when de Forest lived here, the inside matched the outside: wooden panels and screens, exotic furniture, colorful trim in red Agra sandstone and blue Damascus tile. The bronze patterned ceiling flickered with reflections.

One of the balcony's most impressive features has nothing to do with virtuoso artisans or the Orientalizing trends in late 1800s decorative arts – it's just something nature came up with. Although the balcony was carved well over a hundred years ago, the details are still crisp. Teakwood, incredibly tough, is also imbued with oils that protect it from pests and preserve it from the elements.

15.

Patchin Place
Off 10th Street, between Greenwich and 6th Avenues
A, C, E, B, D, F and M trains/West 4th Street
1, 2 and 3 trains/14th Street
L train/6th Avenue

THE LAST GASLIGHT LAMPPOST

A relic from the age of flame

Patchin Place, a tiny gated cul-de-sac off West 10th Street, has been forgotten by the forces of development. It looks more or less like it did 150 years ago. At the street's end, before a painted brick wall, you can find a living fossil: a black cast iron lamppost, complete with crossbar (for propping a ladder) and luminaire, and topped by a decorative eagle. It's an old gaslight lamp. There used to be tens of thousands just like it in New York City – now there's only one.

The evolution of street lighting in New York nicely mirrors the evolution of lighting technology. At the beginning the city's streets flickered with flame. In 1697, fed up with "the great Inconveniency" in the "Darke time of ye moon," the city council ordered residents on busy streets to put lamps in their windows. Oil-burning lamps on wooden posts were used from just before the Revolution, and gaslight followed half a century later. The cast-iron post of the sort you can see in Patchin Place – fluted 8-foot-tall base, octagonal luminaire – was introduced in the 1860s, and soon spread everywhere.

The reign of fire ended in 1880. Electricity has come to define the night: for us, it's the anemic orange of high-pressure sodium lamps. We have to reach back to contemporary accounts to relive the effect of electricity on those accustomed to flame. In 1883, British journalist W.E. Adams compared electric light on Broadway to the moon, to fairy light, to hoar frost. He noted the novelty of stark shadows of tree branches printed on the sidewalk. "The effect of the light in the square of the Empire City can scarcely be described," he wrote, "so weird and so beautiful it is."

Today the lone gaslight lamppost in Patchin Place is fitted with a fluorescent bulb: a cross of old and new. Modern replica lampposts of the same sort – also using electric bulbs – were planted in nearby Washington Square during the recent renovation. "It's so charming," one detractor sitting on the back of a bench said, pausing from rolling his cigarette to twiddle the scornful quotes in the air. "I'm here since I was born, and this place used to have character. Now look."

16.

110 7th Avenue
1 and 2 trains/Christopher Street

THE HESS SPITE TRIANGLE

New York City's smallest piece of private property

In the sidewalk on the corner of Seventh Avenue and Christopher Street is a 300-square-inch mosaic parcel widely considered to be New York City's smallest piece of private property, and also arguably its most slyly vindictive. The Hess Triangle elevates spite to an art form: The tiny, three-sided spit of sidewalk exists solely for the purpose of vengeance.

The origin story of this strange pavement plaque starts in the early 20th century, when the City of New York used eminent domain to claim and clear dozens of area buildings to make way for an extension of Seventh Avenue and the subway below it. Getting to Midtown from lower Manhattan is now significantly easier as a result, but building owners at the time were incensed that their private property was being ripped from their possession for the sake of a private IRT line.

Perhaps no one was as upset by this as the heirs of David Hess, owners of a five-story apartment house called "the Voorhis," which was located in the center of the land slated for destruction – they fought the city tooth and nail to save the address from demolition. Despite their attempts, City Hall was the victor, and by 1914 the Voorhis had been condemned – except for the plot's easternmost portion which, due to sloppy surveyor error, technically remained the property of the Hess estate. The city asked that the incensed heirs donate the uselessly tiny tract and allow it to become public sidewalk, but they refused. Instead, in July 1922, the heirs cemented the corner into local legend with the installation of a mosaic which reads "Property of the Hess Estate which has never been dedicated for public purposes."

Just over a decade later, in 1938, the Hess estate sold their triangle for $100 to the next-door cigar shop, which was purchased (along with the triangle) by Yeshiva University, and then 70 Christopher Realty Corporation. The triangle still lives on in the pavement, its tile now cracked but its message still clear; an old emblem of downtown's prevailing refusal to conform to either societal norms or the street grid. "The 100-year-old Hess Triangle could be said to represent everything about the Village's iconoclasm," says a Village Preservation executive director, calling it a "nearly century-old tribute to one quixotic effort to resist the march of time, and to the idiosyncratic street pattern which defines the Village."

TTE
TTE
Carry on!
WARNING: This product contains nicotine. Nicotine is an addictive chemical.
PROPERTY OF THE
HESS ESTATE
WHICH HAS NEVER
BEEN DEDICATED
FOR PUBLIC
PURPOSES

17.

360 West 11th Street
palazzochupi.com
1 and 2 trains/Christopher Street

PALAZZO CHUPI

A palazzo atop a former horse stable

Ask the average New Yorker to design their own apartment on a limitless budget, chances are they would come up with something a tenth as fantastic as Julian Schnabel's real digs in the West Village. People love it or hate it, but the Palazzo Chupi blazes with what hardly exists anywhere in the city: real whimsy.

Schnabel, most recently famous for his Oscar-nominated direction of *The Diving Bell and the Butterfly*, and famous well before that for his painting and sculpture, can hardly be blamed for knowing what he likes. At the Palazzo Chupi he perched an oversized Venetian palazzo atop a former horse stable in the West Village and painted it radioactive scarlet. Then he filled the place with beautiful things: sculpted fireplaces, Moroccan tile, timbered ceilings, dozens of works of art, and a 40-foot basement pool. The singleness of aesthetic purpose has become a selling point. "Every element and detail in this extraordinary new building [was] created and designed by Mr. Schnabel," claims the realtor's promotional video. It's not just a place to live. It's a "residential work of art."

For many neighbors, it's something of a graphic nightmare. They hate the color, they hate the incongruity, they hate the name. "I have no idea what 'chupi' means," said Andrew Berman to the Villager, "unless it means 'big, ugly building that never should have been built.'" Berman is the director of the Greenwich Village Society for Historic Preservation, and his beef with Schnabel goes beyond personal: it's a matter of taste.

"He's obviously trying to pretend that this looks somehow Florentine or Venetian, when, really, it looks like a Malibu Barbie house that exploded or something." If Berman strikes you as a man unaccustomed to getting exactly what he wants from life, he's one voice in a chorus: after construction began in 2005, demonstrators gathered outside the building site to protest. Schnabel, who currently lives in the palazzo, met the uproar with ego intact. "In principle, the protesters are right," he's quoted saying in Vanity Fair, "but they're wrong about me and this building."

18.

14th St/8th Avenue subway station,
stairway leading down to the L train platform

"MONEYBAGS"

The Boss underground

The "Moneybags" statue in the 14th Street/Eighth Avenue subway station is one part of a vast public art project, Life Underground, on permanent exhibition here since 2001. "Moneybags" caps the railing of a landing on the stair between the A-C-E and L lines, and if there's any foundation to local lore, rubbing the statue as you pass will make you lucky with money. Or at least put you in a frame of mind to make sound decisions about money. Or spice your poverty with ironic wish fulfillment. Or just embarrass you in front of your date. Whatever the reason, people do it: "Moneybags" is always buffed to a high shine.

Experiencing Life Underground for the first time can be the right kind of confusing. One minute you're scurrying along, just another subway rider with somewhere better to be, and the next you're surrounded by surreal, pudgy characters of bronze purposefully going about their business. Tom Otterness, the work's creator, has said that his subject is "the impossibility of life in New York." Impossible, but going on, day after day. There are dozens of vignettes: cops, cleaning ladies, families, businessmen, gentlemen, rogues, as well as inscrutable animals and mystery objects (top prize: a howling bell with a tongue for a clapper). Most compelling about the work is how unwanted the human viewer's attention seems to be here. The bronze figures don't try to teach us any lessons: they are far too absorbed in their own dramas of power, authority, and work to bother with us at all.

The exception is "Moneybags." He stands with his hands clasped behind his back, and appears to maintain a dreamy surveillance of the hustling throng. He's at once smug, menacing, vulnerable, lofty, and weirdly adorable. He also has an antecedent: the character is based on caricatures of corrupt Tammany leader William "Boss" Tweed by the brilliant cartoonist Thomas Nast. Tweed embezzled tens of millions of dollars in taxpayer money, and his public feud with Nast, who largely invented the American political cartoon, made for good copy in the 1870s.

THE "BRAINS"

THAT ACHIEVED THE TAMMANY VICTORY AT THE ROCHESTER DEMOCRATIC CONVENTION.

FROM 14TH TO 42ND

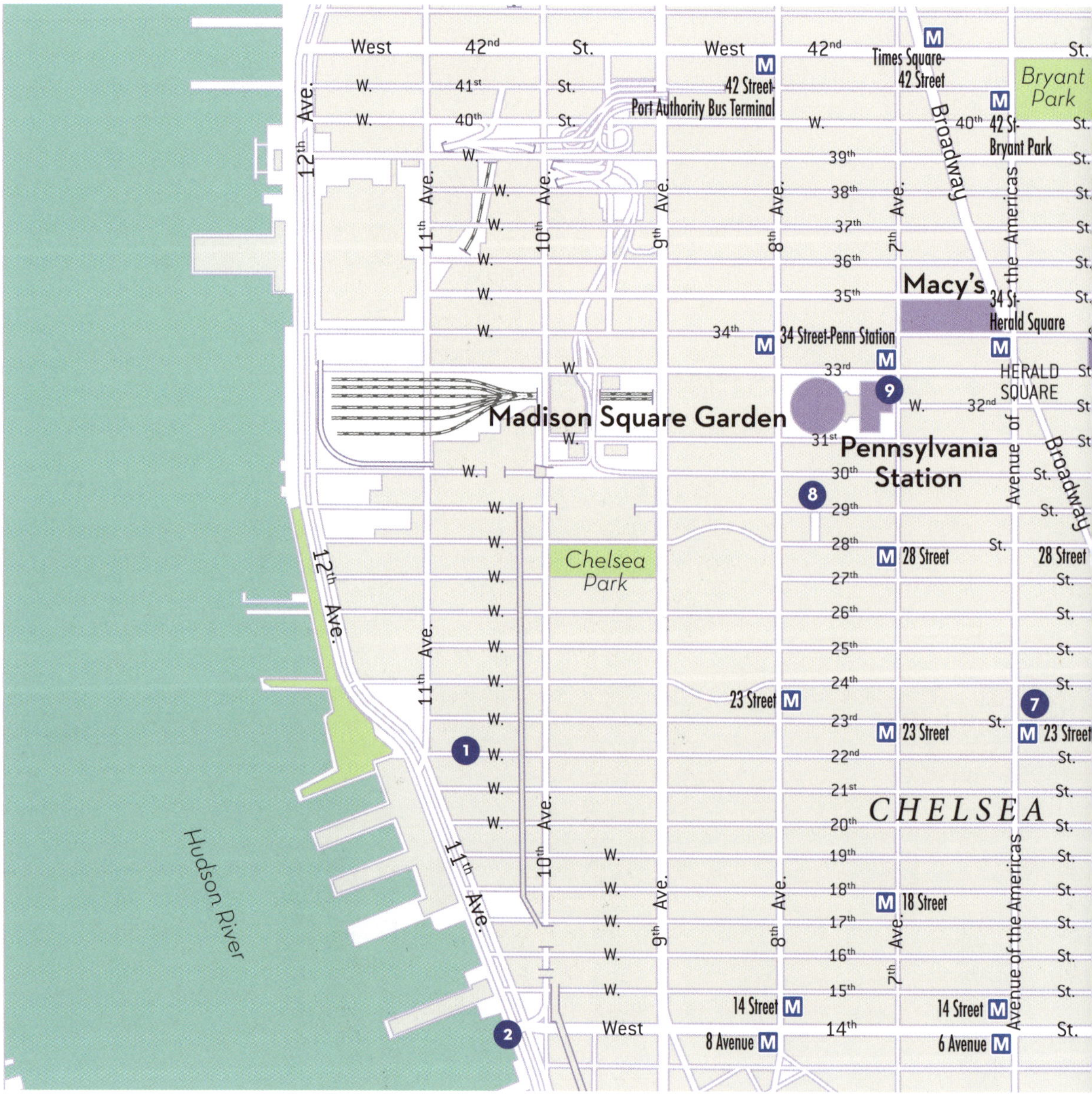

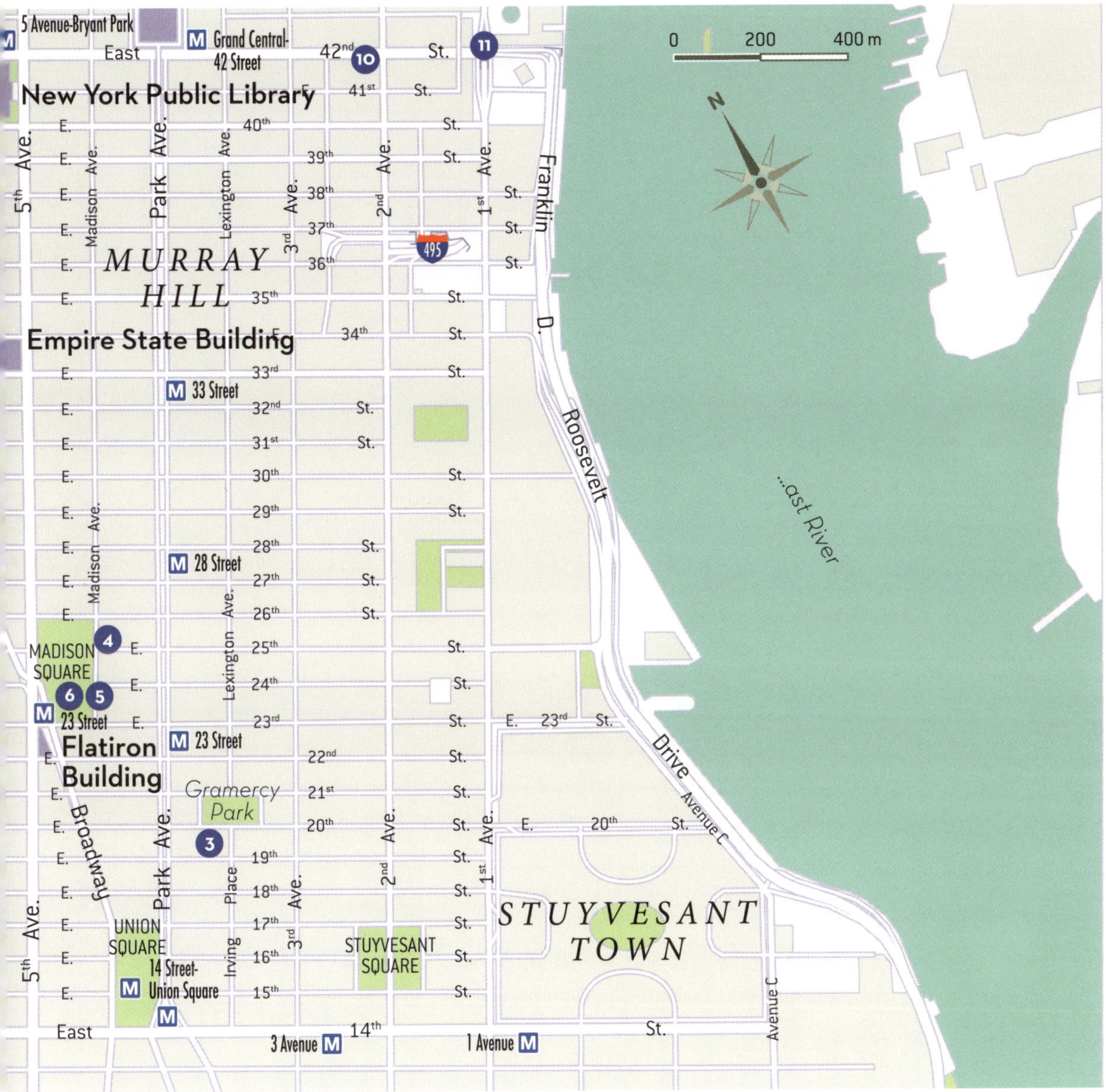
5 Avenue-Bryant Park
Grand Central-42 Street
New York Public Library
MURRAY HILL
Empire State Building
33 Street
28 Street
MADISON SQUARE
23 Street
Flatiron Building
Gramercy Park
UNION SQUARE
14 Street-Union Square
STUYVESANT SQUARE
3 Avenue
1 Avenue
STUYVESANT TOWN
Franklin D. Roosevelt Drive
...ast River
Broadway
5th Ave.
Madison Ave.
Park Ave.
Lexington Ave.
3rd Ave.
2nd Ave.
1st Ave.
Irving Place
Avenue C
0 200 400 m
N

01.

22nd Street between 10th and 11th Avenues
A, C and E trains/23rd Street

"7000 OAKS"

The transformation of all life, on 22nd Street

"7000 Oaks" by German artist Joseph Beuys is a collection of basalt pillars, each installed next to its own tree, lining a whole block of 22nd Street. The work is deliberately quiet, almost secretive. Beuys's goal in art, as far as it can be summarized, was to trigger a spiritual response in people, to remake the world as a great forest. He also took the long view: the trees were planted as saplings, but the artist thought they would create "a very strong visible result in 300 years."

The trees and their stones line both sides of the street. They weren't put there by Beuys himself: "7000 Oaks", installed after his death, is an extension of a much more ambitious project of the same name in the town of Kassel, Germany.

The first tree was planted there by the artist in 1982, the 7000th by his son Wenzel five years later. Most of the trees are oaks, to which Beuys was particularly attracted ("it has always been a form of sculpture, a symbol for this planet") but there are also chestnut, gingko, ash, maple, walnut. Each tree received an enigmatic marker: a basalt column around four feet high. Basalt is born in volcanoes, and can spontaneously create columnar forms, sometimes with uncanny regularity like, Beuys said, "perfect, beautiful organ pipes." Each planting is an event that marks the transformational connections between ecology, society, and life in general. The tree grows; the stone, if it changes at all, can only grow smaller through weathering. The relationship between tree and marker is thus continually evolving, and it's the change that is the real subject of the work.

This is not necessarily a pitch that the Chelsea crowd finds readily audible. One of the more engaging aspects of "7000 Oaks" is how unframeable, how uncollectible, how unsellable it is. Dia Art Foundation, which financed the original project in Kassel, started installing this extension in 1988 on 22nd Street, where it keeps its main offices.

Now the work is very much a part of the neighborhood. "You mean it's ... a thing?" says a smoking man in a delivery uniform, and he shrugs himself off the basalt marker as though it has become suddenly electric.

02.

Under Little Island at Pier 55
between 13th and 14th Street in Hudson River Park

THE REMAINS OF PIER 54

The would-be destination of the Titanic

Over 112 years after the most famous shipwreck in history, all that remains of the vessel's intended destination is tens of rotting wooden posts in the Meatpacking District.

On April 10, 1912, the RMS Titanic set sail from Southampton, England on its maiden voyage, bound for New York City's Pier 59. But of course, the purportedly "unsinkable" ship never did arrive, and only her lifeboats ever made it to Pier 59, dropped off there days late by the rescue vessel RMS Carpathia, which subsequently went south, bringing those spared the Atlantic's icy waters to Pier 54, where thousands warily waited to learn if their loved ones were among the living.

Once one of the numerous Chelsea Piers which lined Manhattan's west side, Pier 54 experienced more than its fair share of prominent wrecks: Three years after hosting the Titanic survivors' grievous homecoming, the ocean liner RMS Lusitania – briefly the biggest passenger ship on Earth – launched from Pier 54 on what would be her final trans-Atlantic crossing. From the pier, the Lusitania, with almost 2,000 passengers, sailed north to Liverpool, never getting past Ireland: On May 7, 1915, a German submarine torpedoed the vessel, sinking it, killing 1,195 of its passengers and becoming the cause of such public outcry that the incident was considered a significant reason the U.S. entered World War I two years later.

Then, in the small hours of May 6, 1932, catastrophe came for the pier itself when a trash fire beneath it grew into a roaring inferno. It took 800 firemen to control the blaze, and by the time it was out, Pier 54 was no more. In time, it was rebuilt, and the decades passed. Then, decay set in. In 1991, Pier 54's crumbling superstructure was demolished; in 2015, its concrete slab went too, to make way for the public park Little Island. Today, all that remains of the once grand pier is its steel archway, still emblazoned with the faded words "Cunard White Star," and, on the park's southern side, an array of mostly submerged wooden pilings, left to create a habitat for aquatic life. For those who happen to look down near the arch, a small round plaque offers a glimpse into the site's history, telling the story of the Titanic in brief beneath the words "The Unsinkable Ship."

THE
UNSINKABLE SHIP
The first years of the 20th
century marked the heyday of luxury
transatlantic ocean liners, but also
witnessed their most infamous disasters.
In 1912, these piers were the intended
destination for the maiden voyage of the
Titanic. After an iceberg in the
North Atlantic, the ship quickly sank and
the lives of most passengers and crew
were lost. The 710 survivors rescued
by the passenger ship Carpathia
were brought to Pier 54 where
these piles stand today.

03.

16 Gramercy Park South
theplayersnyc.org
4, 6, N and R trains/23rd Street
4, 5, 6, N, Q, R and L trains/Union Square

THE PLAYERS

Where Hamlet lived and died

In Gramercy Park stands a bronze statue of Edwin Booth, New York's most famous Shakespearean. To see it, you have to know someone who has a key, or peer through the iron fence, or climb over – Gramercy is Manhattan's only private park. But there's a better way to get to know the actor: arrange a tour of The Players, the nearby gentlemen's club that Booth founded.

"In the 19th century if you thought Hamlet you thought Edwin Booth," says Players librarian Ray Wemmlinger, "and if you thought Edwin Booth you thought Hamlet." Today, of course, if you think Edwin Booth you think the brother of John Wilkes Booth, the man who murdered Abraham Lincoln (see page 74). This theatrical connection is one of the strangest aspects of the tragedy. John Wilkes was an actor, as were his brothers Junius and Edwin. The assassination took place in a theater, and after shooting the president John Wilkes jumped onto the stage and delivered what can only be called a line: "*Sic semper tyrannis!*" ("Thus always with tyrants.")

It's a mark of Edwin's fame that his career survived the crime of his crazed brother. Edwin was so respected, in fact, he raised the station of actors in general. "In 1888 Booth brought together a group of gentlemen," says Wemmlinger, "who were prominent not just in the theater but in a number of different professions. These fellows became the founders and the incorporators of The Players." So Booth helped lift the "rogues and vagabonds" stigma against actors, creating at the same time something like America's only museum of the theater. Downstairs at The Players are elegant drawing rooms; upstairs is the nation's best collection of 19th-century plays, journals, letters, prompt books, and cabinet photos. There is also the virtually untouched bedroom where Edwin Booth lived (and died). It's a trove of memorabilia: a sword used in Macbeth, a leather pouch from *The Merchant of Venice* – even the real human skull the actor used for Hamlet. "Anyone who's involved with the theater is extremely impressed by this room," Wemmlinger says, with understatement.

Booth had three Hamlet skulls, all real. The one at The Players once belonged – in the closest sense – to a convicted horse thief.

The Booth brothers only appeared on stage together once, in Julius Caesar. The performance was a fundraiser for the statue of Shakespeare in Central Park (see page 174).

04.

Manhattan Appellate Courthouse
27 Madison Avenue
N and R trains/23rd Street

APPELLATE COURT HOLOCAUST MEMORIAL

The gates of hell on Madison Square

Although it's 38 feet high and incised with sweeping flames, this memorial to the Holocaust on the west side of the Appellate Courthouse generally goes unnoticed. In many respects the camouflage is intentional; Harriet Feigenbaum, the memorial's creator, carefully chose a marble that would blend well with the architecture. Also, she thought her stark subject matter called not for broad symbolism, but hard, simple facts. This is a sculpture you need to get close to and read to understand.

The focus of the work is what Feigenbaum calls "a photograph interpreted in stone." While hunting in the photo collection in the main branch of the New York Public Library, she came across an aerial view of Auschwitz taken during an Allied bombing raid on August 25, 1944 – a full five months before Auschwitz was finally liberated. "I saw that photo," she says, "and immediately knew it was the one." She was struck by the cold precision there, the detached bird's-eye view of atrocity. The inscription to appear along with the sculpture had already been determined by the memorial committee: *Indifference to Injustice Is the Gate to Hell.* The photo stresses not so much the implicit injustice against the 11 million human beings killed in Nazi concentration camps as the consequences of failing to stop it. Feigenbaum spent six months in Italy refining her carving and selecting marble for the stone photograph and the tall column that rises above it. The theme is reinforced by the column's flames, which drift toward the courthouse – the seat of justice – threatening to engulf it.

The memorial was unveiled in May, 1990. It's interesting to note that a dozen years later former senator and 1972 presidential candidate George McGovern made a public statement about American failure to bomb the railroads and gas chambers of Auschwitz, the horrors of which the Allies had learned from escapees. The failure affected McGovern personally: he was an Air Force pilot during the war, and bombed targets only 5 miles from the camp. "God forgive us," he said, "for that tragic miscalculation."

INDIFFERENCE TO INJUSTICE
EXECUTION WALL
TORTURE CHAMBER
COMMANDANT'S HOUSE
GAS CHAMBER AND CREMATORIUM
IS THE GATE TO HELL

05.

1 Madison Avenue
N and R trains/23rd Street

METROPOLITAN LIFE TOWER

The Venice connection

There is a persistent but overlooked connection between Manhattan and Venice, Italy. Both are island cities, where the streets are corridors and the tightly packed buildings expand upward rather than outward. Both Venice and Manhattan have a Guggenheim Museum and a Harry's Bar (called Harry Cipriani here, it is, according to the owner of both establishments, "almost an exact duplicate of the original"). Gondolas, piloted by gondoliers wearing straw hats and stripes, have always floated among the rowboats on the Lake of Central Park. Recently artist Julian Schnabel reinforced the theme when he suspended his bright pink palazzo in the middle of Greenwich Village (see page 104).

The most visible nod to Venice in New York City is the elegant Metropolitan Life Tower. Rising fifty stories above Madison Square, the tower was completed in 1909, when it became the tallest building in the world. This was still the dawn of skyscrapers; a Times article announcing the tower plan uses language that wobbles like a newborn fawn. "It will go more than 500 feet into the air," the writer promises, and have "offices in it, and elevators running up to the top."

Architects Napoleon Le Brun & Son sought design tips and inspiration in the world's existing towers; the one eventually chosen as the MetLife model was Venice's Campanile in St. Mark's Square.

Also that city's tallest building, the Campanile lorded over the Venetian lagoon for hundreds of years before a spectacular collapse in 1902. Rebuilt over the next decade to exactly match the original, the Campanile now lords again. Here the twinning of New York and Venice becomes something more than symbolic: not only are the outline and proportions the same, construction of Venice's Campanile and its New York mimic took place at the same time.

But why reach into the musty past for engineering tips at all, especially from towers prone to collapse? "The problem for the architects in a building of this sort is harder than the engineering problem," the old *Times* article points out. "It is hard to make such a building, particularly if the base is square, look like anything but a big box on end." You can say that again. And again. And again.

06.

Madison Square Park, south end
nycgovparks.org
N and R trains/23rd Steet

THE ROSCOE CONKLING MONUMENT

The Great Blizzard of 1888

The southernmost monument in Madison Square Park is the model of simplicity: a bronze gentleman, making a vague gesture with his right arm, and ROSCOE CONKLING chiseled in the stone under him. The name might be unfamiliar. U.S. congressman and senator Conkling led the Republican Party during the Grant presidency, but today he's less often remembered for his accomplishments in life than the freak circumstances of his death. Conkling battled the Great Blizzard of 1888, and lost.

The blizzard is the most famous in American history. During the night of Sunday, March 11, a cold front swept over the rainy city; the rain became sleet and then gales of snow that shook buildings and shattered windows. By Monday morning all trains in and out of New York had stopped. Roscoe Conkling left his home on 29th Street and, like on any other weekday, headed downtown to his Wall Street office. The weather went from fierce to berserk: "It seemed as if a million devils were loose in the air," reported the *Herald*. Pedestrians were blown down flat and tossed against buildings; the wind, according to the Sun, "rose and fell and corkscrewed and zigzagged and played merry havoc with everything it could swing or batter or bang or carry away." In some places the snowdrifts were 30 feet deep.

These were the conditions when 58-year-old Conkling, who had sat alone in his office all day, finally buttoned his coat and headed back uptown. His goal was the New York Club on 25th Street; the politician trudged the howling streets to Union Square, where he became suddenly blinded and disoriented. It took him an hour to locate north and forge a path through the snow, finally arriving at the threshold of the club – where he promptly fell flat. Conkling never recovered, and died of pneumonia a month later.

Friends put up the money for this statue by John Quincy Adams Ward. The proposed site was Union Square, but park commissioners thought Madison was more appropriate. The simple monument has stood here since 1893.

07.

71 West 23rd Street
nymasons.org
F and M trains/23rd Street
N and R trains/East 23rd Street – Broadway

GRAND LODGE OF THE FREEMASONS

A very open secret society

The Grand Lodge of New York was once the largest Freemason lodge in the world. Founded in 1782 (although Freemasonry in colonial America goes back further), its current location is, very surprisingly, a nineteen-story building on busy 23rd Street.

So many important figures have been Freemasons, the group has a hazy and sinister reputation for world domination. This makes them inclined to be more accommodating than most institutions. On the 14th floor there's the Masonic library. Along with a maquette of King Solomon's Temple (central to lodge ceremonies) and busts and portraits of prominent Masons (fourteen U.S. presidents, including George Washington), the library features an elaborate facsimile of the *Processus Contra Templarios*, a record of the fourteenth-century Vatican trial against the Knights Templar. There's no proof of a connection between these Knights and the Freemasons but, says director Thomas Savini, "We have the trial here because so many people think there is." It's like an exhibit on the finger of god in a museum of natural history. Savini is smart enough not to let the crazies bug him. "We get all kinds," he says. "We get people who think we're trying to take over the world and want to know where the treasure is. As long as they're careful with the books and respectful of our house rules, they're welcome to come in." The library is a powerful resource: over 60,000 books, one of the largest collections of Freemasonry material in the world.

To form an even more complete idea of New York Masons, visit the lodges on the lower floors. The tour is very – some might say suspiciously – open to the public. Within minutes of escaping the rush of 23rd Street you can be in one of the high-ceilinged, plush ceremonial halls – the Ionic Room, the Renaissance Room – listening to the guide's corny jokes. The halls, redecorated in the 1980s, emit a sumptuousness that is a little generic, but partly because except for the period details they're all exactly the same. The underlying theme seems to be "Freemasons Are Not Threatening In Any Way!" Most of the doors are open to you, but this will do less to reassure a certain type of visitor than convince him that the closed ones conceal darker halls stained with sacrificial blood.

08.

242 West 30th Street
1 train/28th Street

STONE FOXES AND THE FUR TRADE

Guards, off duty

July 27, 1933: three men entered 242 West 30th Street, took the passenger elevator to the tenth floor, made their way to the offices, and pulled out guns. They herded the bookkeeper and owners into a large factory space, where a dozen workers were cutting fox pelts. Two of the men tied the employees up while a third, who "appeared to understand fur values," crammed the choicest pieces into cardboard boxes. The thieves took the freight elevator down and made off with $15,000 worth of furs.

November 21, 1935: two loan sharks, Samuel Mintz and Maxwell "Kitty" Nathan, were convicted of operating a lending business without a license. They targeted the fur trade and they were good at it, depositing up to $100,000 a month. The two proved difficult to prosecute because Mintz was popular among furriers. One, Joseph Fund, admitted to taking out three $100 loans at 5 per cent interest; he worked at the Knickerbocker Fur Company, located at 242 West 30th Street.

February 22 1936: a woman walking down West 30th Street was passing number 242 when she was nearly killed by a large object smashing next to her on the curb. The object was Andrew Turkchensky, 39, who "either fell or jumped six stories to his death." He was a fur cutter and worked in the building.

December 31, 1936: the offices of furriers Cutler & Ostrowsky on the sixth floor of 242 were having a New Year's Eve party. Four bandits broke in, locked the celebrating workers in a stockroom before ransacking the show floor for "mink coats and a large number of Persian lamb skins" valued at more than $10,000.

You're becoming aware of a theme. In the span of a couple of years, all these dramatic stories occurred at the same building; all were reported in the New York Times. Bandits, tragedies, accidents, mobsters, gunmen: it's just a glimpse of the roaring fur trade that defined the neighborhood in the 1920s and 1930s.

Constructed in 1927, 242 West 30th is decorated by two very serious and emblematic stone foxes, a tribute to the countless animals that were exploited here for their skins. The foxes made, as you may have noticed, lousy guards.

For another, weirder architectural relic of the fur trade, try one block south at 214 West 29th, where stone gnomes fondle squirrels and pelts with a longing that borders on pornographic.

242

09.

7th Avenue at West 33rd and West 31st Streets
1, 2 and 3 trains/34th Street – Penn Station

THE EAGLES OF OLD PENN STATION

One entered the city like a god

Two stone eagles stand on Seventh Avenue in front of Penn Station, one at 33rd Street and the other at 31st. Nearly 6,000 pounds of solid marble each, they claw their granite plinths with chest out and wings up, staring puzzledly at the passing traffic. If the eagles seem a little off, it's because although they're in roughly the right place, they're in the wrong time. Once part of the imperial facade of the beloved old Penn Station, the birds are now grounded in front of the despised new one, and their presence feels more like an insult than a tribute.

Architects and historians talk about the original Penn Station like they would about a murdered relative. "How tragic, how sad," said historian David McCullough in the documentary New York, "that so many Americans will never know what it was like to arrive in New York for the first time in your life at Penn Station." The waiting hall was the largest indoor space in the city, with coffered vaults and Corinthian columns modeled after the Caracalla baths of ancient Rome. Outside rose a perimeter colonnade 35 feet high; there were entrances on all four sides – a first for railway stations – and above each hung a great clock wreathed in stone and flanked by allegorical figures of Night and Day. When it was finished in 1910, architects McKim Mead & White thought they'd built a metropolitan temple for the ages.

The old Penn stood for only fifty-three years. Jets and highways spelled the end of the train era; in 1962 the Pennsylvania Railroad, weary of operating costs, announced plans to raze the Beaux-Arts treasure and replace it with Madison Square Garden, which on its best day looks like a Soviet uranium enrichment facility. The rail system was damned to a subterranean maze at the same location. Yale University professor Vincent Scully summed it up: "One entered the city like a god; one scuttles in now like a rat."

It took workmen more than three years to smash up the acres of carved granite and travertine. Sculptor Adolph Weinman's stonework – capitals, angels, allegories – was piled into a swamp in New Jersey. The eagles that stare at Seventh Avenue today bear no plaque to explain their past, and canvassing the Penn Station area reveals that practically none of the security guards, hotel clerks, office workers, friendly drunks, ticket sellers or ticket scalpers have ever noticed them.

10.

220 East 42nd Street
4, 5, 6, 7 and S trains/Grand Central – 42nd Street

DAILY NEWS BUILDING LOBBY

A 4,000-pound globe at the center of the world

The great Art Deco buildings in the city have a heroic quality that's been missing ever since. Rockefeller Center, the Empire State, the Chrysler. They have what you might call unembarrassed grandeur. Add to this list a structure that is less visited, but features an attraction that resonates with the 1930's mindset: the Daily News Building and the titanic 4,000-pound globe in its lobby. The globe is sunk into the floor, and lit dramatically from below through tiers of frosted glass. The impression is one of quiet, unstrained power: if the glowing sphere turned out to provide a mysterious energy that permeates the entire building, you would not find this totally surprising. On the polished brass and terrazzo floor around it spread dark jags, like the wind bearings on an ancient compass rose; above rises a recessed canopy of angular black glass. The Daily News used this address as headquarters from 1929 to 1995, and counterbalancing the idealism is a sense of the hustle and nerve of a major international newspaper. In case the message was lost on anyone, set into the floor in brass are place names followed by a number: Johannesburg: 7988, Bermuda: 768 – the distances in miles from New York City, the center of the world. But also in the floor are facts meant to expand the mind: "If the Sun were the SIZE of this GLOBE," reads one, "the EARTH would be the Size of a WALNUT and Located at the Main Entrance to Grand Central Terminal."

In the same spirit of cosmic precision, the gigantic planet has been mounted, at untold extra hassle, to the proper tilt of the Earth. And it moves. Regularly, like a ticking clock, the whole ball revolves a few degrees on its axis. Vernon, the man behind the lobby desk, has worked next to the globe for decades but still seems a little in awe of it. "If you go all the way in, you'll see: that's hand-painted. They didn't fool around with all this other crazy stuff," waving his hand to impugn modernity in general. "Somebody actually *painted* that."

SUPERMAN'S NEWSPAPER

Fans of Superman will recognize the Daily News Building as the setting for the Daily Planet, the newspaper of Clark Kent and Lois Lane in the Richard Donner film of 1978. The Daily Planet Building first appears in animations of the DC Comic in 1942; the inspiration may have been the globe-topped Paramount Building in Times Square.

11.

Visible on any cross street in the grid above 14th Street, usually on May 28 and July 12

MANHATTAN SOLSTICE

When the Solar System aligns with the grid

When the Commissioners' Plan of 1811 laid the city grid system, the streets were made to follow Manhattan's natural axis. The island is tilted 29 degrees from plumb, a fact that often puzzles New Yorkers when, after a daily life of subway and city plans oriented to the geometry of the grid, they see Manhattan on a map where New York is no longer the center of the universe. It's one of the city's ironies that a street plan so rigidly defined by the cardinal directions is actually more than just a little off.

Twenty-two days on either side of the summer solstice (usually June 21), New Yorkers get an awesome reminder that Manhattan is just a spot on a spinning globe locked into orbit around a star. On these days the sun sets directly in line with the cross streets. The event has been given the name Manhattanhenge, hinting at ancient mysteries, but part of the beauty is a lack of design – or better, how neatly the Solar System seems to have annexed a design conceived for a different purpose. Every town on Earth has a sunset, and streets, but only New York is an island city made up of measured canyons and titanic buildings.

You can observe the event on any cross street, but it's most spectacular where the buildings are huge – 42nd Street has become the favorite.

And you have to go to the extreme east side of the island to get the full effect of the sun threading the needle. Because it spans 42nd, the Tudor City Bridge is the only place you can get a clear view without dodging traffic.

By 8 o'clock, a small but dedicated crowd has gathered. "Here it goes," someone says, as the sun tracks from the left into the gleaming corridor, and the chink of sky ahead, already washed in orange, suddenly flames gold. The bridge chitters with the sound of cameras while the sun, strangely magnified, inches down the gap. Then it's gone: the sky fades to peach, grading into violet where it meets the airy silhouette of New Jersey. Down below a police car squawks at a ragged group squinting into the last flush of color: "Get out of the middle of the street!"

In winter Manhattanhenge occurs again, but flipped: evenly spaced on either side of the winter solstice (usually December 21), the sun rises at the eastern end of cross streets.

FROM 42ND TO 59TH

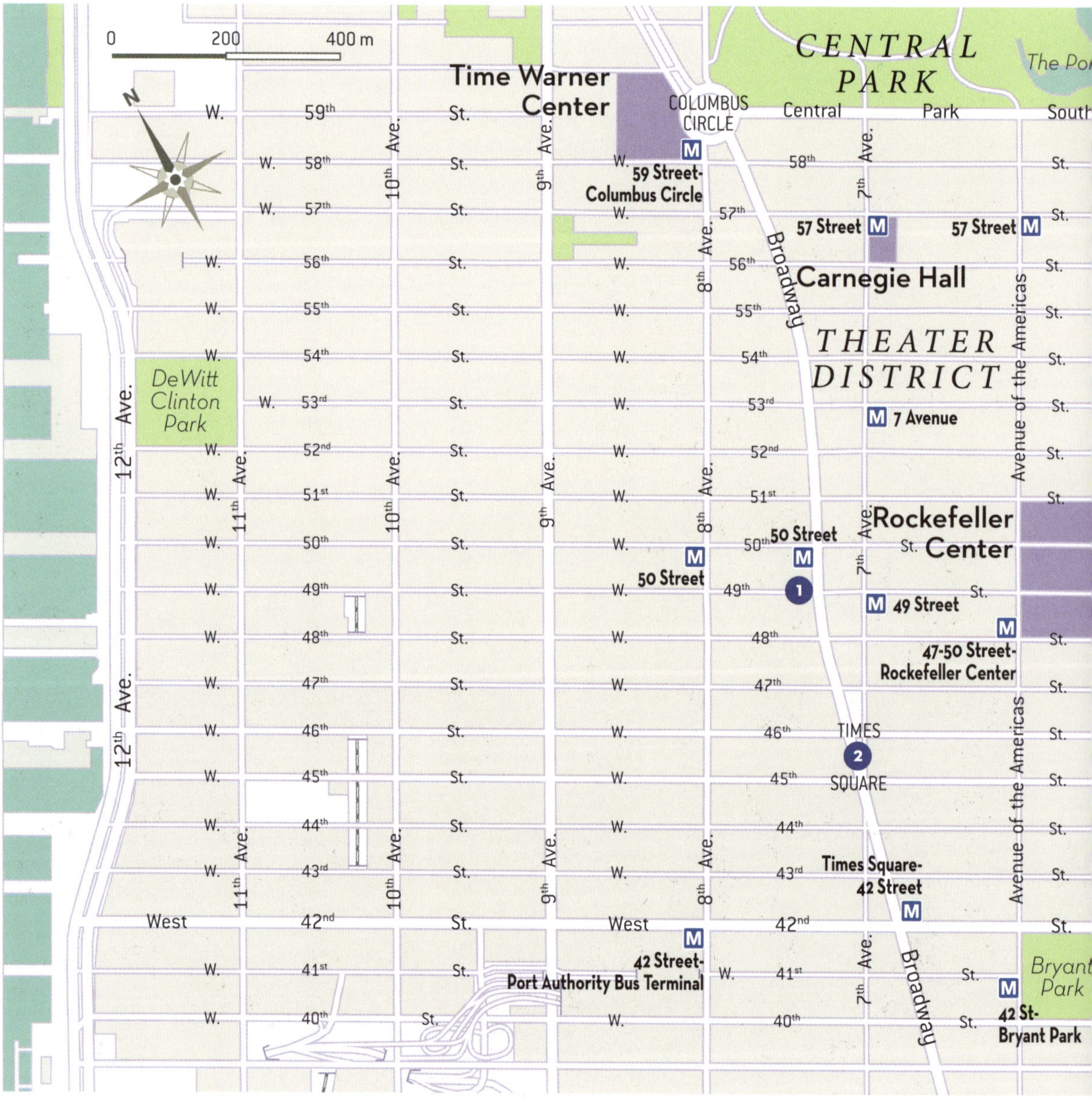

01. THE BRILL BUILDING *p. 134*

02. TIMES SQUARE SOUND SCULPTURE *p. 136*

03. THE PIG OF SAINT PATRICK'S *p. 138*

04. LEVER HOUSE PLAZA *p. 140*

05. GREENACRE PARK *p. 142*

06. MARILYN MONROE SUBWAY GRATE *p. 144*

5 Avenue / 59 Street
M
Lexington Avenue/ 59 Street
M
59 Street
M
East 59th St.
60th St.
QUEENSBORO BRIDGE
MIDTOWN
5th Ave.
Madison Ave.
Park Ave.
Lexington Ave.
3rd Ave.
2nd Ave.
1st Ave.
York Ave.
E. 58th St.
E. 57th St.
E. 56th St.
E. 55th St.
E. 54th St.
E. 53rd St.
E. 52nd St.
E. 51st St.
E. 50th St.
E. 49th St.
E. 48th St.
E. 47th St.
E. 46th St.
E. 45th St.
E. 44th St.
E. 43rd St.
East 42nd St.
E. 41st St.
E. 40th St.
M 5 Avenue / 53 Street
M
Lexington Avenue / 53 Street
51 Street
M
Saint Patrick's Cathedral
Grand Central
Grand Central-42 Street
M
5 Avenue-Bryant Park
M
Chrysler Building
New York Public Library
Franklin D. Roosevelt Drive
East River
United Nations Headquarters
U Thant Island
3
4
5
6
7
8
9
10
11
12

01.

1619 Broadway at 49th Street
1, 2, A and C trains/50th Street
N, Q and R trains/49th Street

THE BRILL BUILDING

Tragic reversal in Times Square

The area of Times Square steeps in a constant, twitching bath of colorful light: that there might be fascinating buildings behind all that glow is at best an afterthought. In the relative dark of the area's upper end at Broadway and 49th, one unique structure deserves your attention: the Brill Building. It has the only Art Deco facade in the neighborhood, and an odd addition: over the entrance, and again even more imposingly ten stories above the street, you'll find large, lifelike portraits of a young man with a dead gaze. Anyone who's ever wondered why more buildings don't include monumental portraiture, here's your answer: it looks a little strange.

The young man is Alan E. Lefcourt, son of the building's developer. In fact it should be called the Alan E. Lefcourt Building, and the reason it isn't is a tale of tragic reversal. Alan's father Abraham Lefcourt started out as a shoeshine boy and worked his way up, in true metropolis fashion, to the top of a realty empire. He was devoted to his only son; on the boy's 13th birthday he gave him a Midtown skyscraper, and named this building on 49th after him. That name was soon going to be known throughout the world: drawn up in 1929 when Lefcourt was worth around $100 million, the Times Square building was, on paper, the tallest anywhere. Then in the space of a couple of years Lefcourt's boy died of anemia, the stock market crashed, the building got downscaled, investors filed lawsuits, the empire crumbled, and Lefcourt himself died, perhaps by his own hand. The brothers who leased the property foreclosed, and put their own name on it. The Brill Building would go on to be a pillar of the American music industry.

BIG APPLE CORNER

Five blocks up Broadway on 54th Street, you can see perhaps the only memorial to a nickname. The intersection is officially called Big Apple Corner. The origin of the term "the Big Apple" as slang for New York City is a bit foggy, but it seems to be a product of 1930's Black culture. Big Apple was the name of a popular Harlem jazz club; playing there meant being at the top of your game. The term was also used by African- American stable boys at the racetrack, where it was heard by sports columnist John FitzGerald, who then popularized it in the press. Big Apple Corner is near the hotel where FitzGerald lived and eventually died.

BRILL BUILDING
1619
DELIVERIES AT 49TH STREET

02.

Southwest corner of 46th Street and Seventh Avenue,
on the traffic island east of Broadway
1, 2, 3, 7, N, R, Q, S, W trains/42nd Street – Times Square
1 train/50th Street
N, R and W trains/49th Street

TIMES SQUARE SOUND SCULPTURE

"People are not that observant"

"It sounds like some kind of extraterrestrial," smiles John, gazing at his feet in puzzlement. John is from Ghana and he wears the red jacket of the street crew who sell tickets to the tour buses. Times Square is his beat and he works the same corner "every day, all day long." He cocks his head to lower his ear a little through the din of one of the world's most visited places. From the surrounding streets rumble cars and trucks, the ventilation ducts of the building on the other side of Broadway moans, and a thousand languages babble from the high tide of tourists. But at this moment only John is aware for the first time that from underfoot, at this precise point, a distinct but unearthly hum swells endlessly.

This sound sculpture – titled simply "Times Square" – is the work of artist Max Neuman, and it has sung here since 1977. Just what is singing is unclear. If you get on the ground and put your eye to the metal grate, all you see are dirty girders and the urban dandruff you'd expect: bits of paper, bottle caps, the odd coin. It seems the street itself is singing. The effect is something like a huge bell a few seconds after being struck. And while it doesn't change much, the sound is busy with layered tones; it has a vroom in it, like it's continually heading off somewhere.

"It sounds like chimes," says Guy, who a moment before was hustling over the traffic island with his head down, like any New Yorker obliged to cross Times Square. "It's cool that you could live in the city for a long time and still discover new parts of it. Like a treasure map." What is the sound saying? "Maybe that people are not that observant." Or that everywhere is somewhere. This artwork plants a curious flag on a nondescript corner that teems with distraction. Noticing it reminds you, strikingly, of the presence of your own self, right here and now.

2:48
TDK
LISTE

03.

Lady Chapel of Saint Patrick's Cathedral (exterior)
Corner of Madison Avenue and 51st Street
saintpatrickscathedral.org
E and M trains/5th Avenue – 53rd Street
B, D, F and M trains/Rockefeller Center
4 and 6 trains/51st Street

THE PIG OF SAINT PATRICK'S

Comical and unterrifying

Asked if the cathedral has any interesting secrets to tell, the good ladies at the welcome desk of St. Patrick's shake their heads. "No," says Eileen. "No," says Marianne – but then she points a thumb to the rear of the church. "Unless you want to see the pig?"

The "pig" is a stone demon that crawls up the outer wall of the Lady Chapel at the cathedral's back end. For years the sculpture has been an inside joke among St. Patrick's priests, who have a good view of it from their second-story apartments in the rectory a few feet away. It's the first thing they see when they look out in the morning, and nobody knows what it is.

Five minutes later Marianne nods at the sculpture while the traffic blares by on Madison Avenue. The creature doesn't look very much like a pig. It doesn't look like any earthly thing: it's a stubby-armed monster grappling on the arched windows, with three-toed feet, a bulbous abdomen, and a cockscombed neck that disappears into a gap in the stonework.

"Someone thought it was a hippopotamus," says Monsignor Ritchie. He and Father Joe have come to stand at the open rectory window above the sidewalk, their feet about eye-level. The two live upstairs. "Bishop Sullivan thought it looks like it has a duck foot." They say the pig plays no role in the priestly schedule other than obscure fun. "But," says Father Joe, "when I show somebody the cathedral, I tell them to look up there. Nobody's ever seen it, it's one of those little oddities."

Monsters are longstanding companions of churches; some are visitors from Hell. Did it ever occur to the priests that the original intent might not be so playful, that the pig might have some darker business up there? "Playful," Father Joe and Monsignor Ritchie say in smiling unison, nodding their heads.

They're right. The Lady's Chapel is a later addition, built not by chief architect James Renwick but Charles T. Mathews. According to an old cathedral guide book, Mathews lived for a period in France, and acquired "a taste for gargoyles." His original plan called for hideous grotesques, but the trustees made him settle for something more "comical and unterrifying." The gargoyles were removed in the 1940s when they became unstable; the "pig" tucked away in its snug corner was left alone.

04.

390 Park Avenue
E and M trains/5th Avenue – 53rd Street

LEVER HOUSE PLAZA

Big art for working stiffs

The Lever House has always been an icon: it's the first "curtain wall" skyscraper, where the outer shell is hung on a load-bearing structure within. Recently the building has come to notice for a different reason: as an unexpected contemporary art museum.

Constructed in 1950-52, the building was initially the headquarters of British soap manufacturers Lever Brothers. The crystalline slab, 24 stories high, sparked a rage for curtain walls: within ten years, the mile of Park Avenue from Grand Central to 59th Street shimmered with glass. Landmarked in 1982 and restored by real estate company RHR Holding, today the Lever House looks like it did half a century ago. With one compelling difference: the outdoor plaza now features large, even monumental sculptures and installations by prominent artists.

This is thanks to Richard Marshall, a friend of the owners and for 20 years a curator at the Whitney Museum. Originally RHR Holding mulled a commercial application for the spot, but the building's landmark status limited the options. Marshall pushed the idea of an ever-changing exhibition space, where artists would present large sculptural works in the plaza, supplemented by other work in various media in the glass-encased lobby. Now the project is Lever House policy.

Major sculptures by (among many others) Damien Hirst, Keith Haring, and Jeff Koons have been shown here. Artists are attracted by the chance to install their work in a part of town that no one would think to call edgy, and RHR Holding makes gains in the nebulous area of cachet. But it's basically a public service. "Galleries have shows to sell something, and museums ask admissions," notes Marshall. "We don't do either. We don't sell anything. We don't charge anything. And it's open every day." Asked if the art isn't maybe a bit much for the office crowd (for instance, Hirst's 35-foot bronze sculpture Virgin Mother is a pregnant woman with half her skin peeled off), Marshall says, "I hear complaints and I hear compliments."

Cross the street to 375 Park Avenue to visit another icon of functionalist architecture: Mies van der Rohe's 38-story Seagram Building, erected five years after the Lever House.

05.

217 East 51st Street
greenacrepark.org
E and M trains/53rd Street
4 and 6 trains/51st Street

GREENACRE PARK

Manhattan, distilled

New York is dotted with oases: spots where a person can step off the amusement ride of the city for a moment and breathe an air of peace. Many of them occur naturally and are highly personal: a stairwell or a couple of trees might do it. Others are wholly engineered, and of these Greenacre Park on 51st Street is the champion.

The most striking feature is the total rejection of nature. Greenacre makes no effort at *rus in urbe*, the facsimile of countryside. You don't feel like you've left Manhattan so much as entered a space where Manhattan's characteristics have been distilled to the very essence. There is geometry here, and public life, and incessant noise, and the peace on offer is a Manhattan-flavored peace: it's busy and self-aware. The centerpiece is a 25-foot cascade that mimics the tiers of the cityscape: thousands of gallons of water roar continuously over climbing blocks of granite, and on either side the ivy wraps around the underlying stone at right angles. The roar is a calculated effect. Sit in the fine mist of the lower terrace with a book, and the street only a few paces away becomes muted: the constant waterfall static amounts to a kind of silence. The air in the small park even has a pleasant and unnatural scent: a hint of chlorine.

The need for urban oases was officially recognized under Mayor Lindsay with his Vest Pocket park initiative. Sound is a feature of more than one; the use of roaring water to mask the honks and growls of the city has the compelling name "grey noise." Constructed in 1971, Greenacre was paid for by a private institution, and its rules are many and specific: no moving the chairs between terrace levels, no exercising, no touching the plants, no pets. The security guard, who might otherwise pass his time staring at the rushing water in a hypnotic sway, won't hesitate to enforce.

PALEY PARK

Greenacre has a conceptual sister three avenues away: Paley Park on 53rd Street. Paley offers a minimalism that also serves to distill an aspect of Manhattan: with a plain, solid wall of water, and symmetrical files of slender honey locust trees, it's chic. See it in the evening when the cascade is lit from behind with sodium light, and the water blurs and gleams like brushed gold.

06.

Southwest corner of Lexington Avenue and East 52nd Street
4 and 6 trains/51st Street

MARILYN MONROE SUBWAY GRATE

Where the Girl became the Legend

The subway goes by, and air billows through the sidewalk grate, blowing up Marilyn Monroe's skirt. If it's not the most famous moment in American cinema, it's not far down the list. It happened on the corner of Lexington and East 52nd.

Marilyn Monroe was always slated to star in "The Seven Year Itch". In the film (and the Broadway hit it's based on) Monroe's character appears in the script as simply The Girl. The story is straightforward: trusted husband is home alone, Girl tempts him into a frenzy. Director Billy Wilder thought the film might never make it past Hollywood's prudish production code. Eventually he conceded a crucial point: in the play the two eventually wind up in bed together, while in the film the tension is never resolved. Monroe comes out even more desirable for it.

The iconic "subway scene" seems practically wholesome today, but its notoriety endures. Trusted husband (Tom Ewell) and Monroe stroll out of the cinema on a hot summer night. "Oh, here comes the breeze from the subway!" Monroe sings, "Isn't it delicious?" New Yorkers already know the answer to this (No), but who cares? We're in Movieland. The shooting took place on September 9, 1954, and was widely publicized: by the time Monroe arrived in her pleated halter dress, a thousand spectators had gathered, along with a jostling pack of press photographers.

In the same way the husband's upstairs neighbor is simplified as The Girl, so has Monroe's entire film career – her entire person – been compressed into this one moment: bare legs revealed as the subway passes underground. Subway Marilyn posters, Subway Marilyn coffee mugs, tee shirts, key chains, mouse pads, piggy banks: you can find all this in Fifth Avenue trinket shops. But few people make the pilgrimage to Lexington and East 52nd Street. The manager of the restaurant fronted by the legendary grate says that those who do are a little let down. "There's no plaque or sign or anything." Steve McClendon, a sanitation worker who sweeps the grate "twenty or thirty times a day" doesn't know the film, and seems shaky on just who Marilyn Monroe was. After suffering an imitation of the iconic pose, he smiles. "Oh, that," he says, "Yeah, I've seen that."

BUSES
ONLY

07.

Waldorf Astoria
301 Park Avenue
hilton.com/fr/hotels/nycwawa-waldorf-astoria-new-york
4 and 6 trains/51st Steet

THE COLE PORTER PIANO

There's no love song finer, but how strange the change from major to minor

On the Park Avenue mezzanine of the Waldorf Astoria stands a Steinway piano. The top is cracked, the finish is worn, the instrument is silent: a fallboard is locked over the keys. But the piano emanates, like an antenna tuned to nostalgia, the elegance of old New York: dinner jackets, evening dresses, cigarette cases, cocktail parties. It used to belong to Cole Porter.

Porter moved into the Waldorf Towers in 1934, but he began defining New York through his music long before that. Some of his songs draw directly from the city – "Washington Square," "Take Me Back to Manhattan," "I Happen to Like New York" – but there is a general quality in his compositions that seems to express what is romantic and smart and fashionable about urban life. It's the idea of New York without all the details.

The piano was built in 1907. It's a midsize mahogany grand the color of dark honey, with double Empire-style legs and hand-painted garlands and court figures. Porter gave it to the hotel in 1939, but it stayed with him in his apartment suite, arranged curve-to-curve with another piano, until he died in 1964. In a way, the instrument maps the fate of piano song. Putting clever words to chords made Porter a social lion. After his death the piano was moved to the Royal Suite, a baronial luxury apartment that runs the full length of the 50th Street block on the hotel's top floor. Later it filled the Waldorf Astoria central lobby with a kind of classic luxury soundtrack in the Peacock Alley lounge, until finally settling into its spot on the mezzanine directly over the hotel's main entrance on Park Avenue. At some point during this trajectory the piano became the "Cole Porter piano" – that is, a piece of museum furniture. On the mezzanine it was played for fifteen years by Daryl Sherman, one of the best performers of the dying song form. "This is not me playing," she would say before a rendition of "Night and Day" – "This is Cole Porter's spirit playing by Ouija board." When the Waldorf Astoria was bought by the Blackstone Group in 2007, operations were streamlined and Sherman was shown the door. Now the piano mostly stays locked.

Steinway & Sons offers a replica of the Cole Porter grand. It's called the "High Society."

Porter's Waldorf Towers suite, 33A, went on the market in 2010. The rate: $140,000/month.

08.

551 Fifth Avenue at 45th Street
7 train/5th Avenue
S train/Grand Central – 42nd Street

THE FRED F. FRENCH BUILDING

Babylon on Fifth Avenue

Many of New York's Art Deco buildings are beautifully suggestive of Mesopotamia. The design trend has been traced to D.W. Griffith's 1916 film "Intolerance" and its seductive sets, but some taller New York buildings – the "setback" giants that climb the sky in diminishing tiers – look like Bronze Age step pyramids because of an early zoning law. To see the forces of design and regulation at work on a masterpiece of modern Babylon, visit the Fred F. French Building on Fifth Avenue.

The Manhattan setback zoning law was America's first. It ordered that once a structure reached a certain height, it had to step inward from the street. The earliest tall buildings used this model as a matter of structural necessity, but with the metal frame folks worried – with good reason – that sunlight would disappear from the metropolitan sidewalk forever. The French Building illustrates the law: it begins to step back a dozen floors up, until the tower gradually shrinks to 25% of the area of the footprint, at which point it was allowed to go as high as the very vault of heaven. The temple-like profile is in part accidental, but the cladding is Babylonian Art Deco at its purest. The French is flushed with ochre masonry, trimmed in black, and the tower is topped by a vivid frieze in colored faience: griffins flanking a stylized sun. But to get the full flavor of yore, enter the lobby. The entrance is a glowing bronze tribute to the Ishtar Gate, with decoration that is "a most literal evocation of Manhattan as the New Babylon, of the skyscraper as Nebuchadnezzar's hanging garden in the desert" (New York 1930; Stern, Gilmartin and Mellins). The lobby itself is vaulted with gilt mythical animals, leading down to the most stupefying elevator bank in the city. On either side, the polished bronze doors gleam with stylized allegories, as if lifted directly from the throne room of a god-king.

The setback zoning law was in effect in New York from 1916 to 1961.

Sloan & Robertson consulted when the French Building went up in 1926; for another example of their Babylon-enriched architecture from the same period, see page 152.

09.

Grand Central Terminal, 87 East 42nd Street
Dining concourse directly in front of the Oyster Bar & Restaurant

THE WHISPERING GALLERY IN GRAND CENTRAL

Telegraph by Guastavino tile

Grand Central Terminal has an unmarked spot with otherworldly properties: a handsome vaulted ceiling where you can speak softly into one corner and be plainly heard by someone in the opposite corner 40 feet away. The effect is truly uncanny, and cuts through the surrounding din of echoes, whistles and roars of the biggest train station in the world.

There are several buildings in the States and abroad with the architectural quirk that produces the whispering gallery effect; what you need is an unbroken ellipsoid and points of focus directly opposite one another. Grand Central's whispering gallery is just in front of the Oyster Bar & Restaurant, and the pattern of tiled vaults continues inside where staff and patrons still find new sweet spots of particular clarity. For best results, speak facing the corner, as close to the stone as possible. Make sure your cohort is in the diagonally opposite corner, not one next to you. The sound is said to "telegraph" along the vault, and the term is apt: the voice you hear has a spectral, disembodied quality, as though transmitted through some antiquated technology.

Another feature of whispering galleries: they're generally flukes. Perfectly ellipsoidal tile ceilings are certainly not, however – those we owe to the hard work of Spanish-born builder Rafael Guastavino. The architect came to New York from Barcelona with his son in 1881 and soon after patented his "Tile Arch System" of standard-size, interlocking terracotta tiles. The tiles had distinct structural advantages: they were fireproof, and could be applied directly into mortar over long arches and vaults without the need for temporary supports. Although employed in Catalonia for years, the technique was hardly known in the United States. Guastavino and his son eventually filed over twenty patents, and the demand for the arch system became so fierce, tile makers couldn't work fast enough to meet it.

Guastavino tile is a prominent feature of Beaux-Arts New York architecture and can be found in dozens of notable buildings, including the Cathedral Church of St. John the Divine, the Registry Room at Ellis Island, and the Federal Reserve Bank.

VANDERBILT AVENUE 42ND STR
RANT

10.

Lexington Avenue between 43rd and 44th Streets
4, 5, 6, 7 and S trains/Grand Central – 42nd Street

THE GRAYBAR BUILDING RATS

Art Deco pests

Often mistaken for an eastern extension of Grand Central Terminal, the Graybar Building on Lexington Avenue has its own identity, and a pioneering one. After completion in 1927, the brick and limestone headquarters of the Graybar Electric Company became the largest office tower in the world. The facade is aligned to the Assyrian geometries that informed 1920s Art Deco (see page 148), and while the titanic curly-bearded allegories of Transportation and Communication on the east face set a distinctive tone, the building's uniqueness is best expressed lower down, on the struts that hold up the awning. There you'll find New York's only architectural rats.

The rats are easy to miss; it wasn't until 1933 that they came to the attention of the New Yorker. "When plans for the building were being developed," The Talk of the Town reads, "the architects thought they ought to strike the maritime note somewhere in its decorations." This note is found in the bas-relief albatrosses that decorate the facade, but the architects Sloan & Robertson also brilliantly marked a parallel between the awning struts and the hawser lines used for mooring or towing ships. It goes beyond rats: the ones scampering up the front of the Graybar are frustrated by "bafflers" – the funnels that guard real rats from stowing away on ships in harbor.

Made of cast iron, and segmented into angular planes that would appear modern to the Jazz Age passerby but robotic to the modern one, the rats look like they're up to no good. And there are more: each of the iron struts connects to the building at a rosette composed of rat heads.

The Graybar was an A-rated building in its early life, with offices of publishing giants Condé Nast, Vogue, and Vanity Fair, as well as those of Remington typewriters. Over the years the address slipped in status, and one by one the cast-iron varmints disappeared. When the building was restored in 2000, among the special instructions on the technical drawings was the irregular phrase: "Replace missing rats."

11.

320 East 43rd Street (atrium access on 42nd Street)
fordfoundation.org
4, 5, 6 trains and 7 train/Grand Central – 42nd Street

FORD FOUNDATION ATRIUM

A box of forest on 42nd Street

There's no other building in New York City that pulls off a green trick like the one on display at the Ford Foundation. The back entrance is an atrium as tall as the structure itself: twelve stories of open air enclosed on two sides by glass. On the ground – it would be strange to call it the floor – are terraced levels of jungle flora. As you open the door you're aware of a rush of oxygen and the aroma of damp wood, and a whisper in your head: *This is not what I expected to find on 42nd Street.*

To be precise, not all of the plants are of the jungle sort. Lal, a gardener here, says that they are "a mix of tropical and temperate." For an example of temperate he points to a pine; the tropical is most everything else: Lal recognizes many of the types of vegetation that he can see in his native Guyana. The atrium does indeed have the feeling of a parcel of earth quarried from some distant, humid forest. At the same time it's pleasantly neat: swept tile paths cut through the plants, converging at the bottom on a wishing fountain. "We give the coins to UNICEF," says Eddie, a guard who has been at the Foundation thirty years. He says the best time to come – and he should know – is around 10 o'clock in the morning, when the sun slants through the windows from the east.

The atrium is impressive to the eye, but the motive behind the design is deeper than beauty. The Ford Foundation, a legacy of automaker Henry Ford and his son Edsel, is a private charitable corporation; focus issues include poverty, education, and social justice. Architects Kevin Roche and John Dinkeloo recognized that the moral lifeblood of such an organization is transparency. Roche imagined Foundation workers peering out across the open atrium and feeling more aware of their colleagues, everyone connected by a communal sense of responsibility. If the idea sounds oppressive, the reality isn't – or at least not visibly so. The offices with their lighted windows, divided into floors by weathered iron beams, seem to share a purpose with each other, and with the fragrant plant life below.

12.

East River at 42nd Street

U THANT ISLAND

Manhattan's smallest island, and former sovereign nation

In the middle of the East River at about the level of 42nd Street rises a scrubby hump of land with a metal navigation tower. Less than an acre in area, U Thant is Manhattan's smallest island, but it has seen some interesting history.

The island began as a granite outcrop called Man o'War Reef. It was once the scene of a perfectly New York City adventure: in the 1930s, a group of teens trying to swim across the river from Manhattan were forced by the current onto the reef, which then began to disappear as the tide came in. A playwright who was watching the fiasco unfold through binoculars from a tower apartment called the authorities and all the boys – who were by then standing in a foot of water – were saved. When the first Manhattan-Queens tunnel was dug beneath the river for a tram service to the company town of Steinway & Sons (see page 146), excavated rock from Manhattan was piled onto the reef to make it a permanent island, and a hundred-foot shaft was sunk straight down to branch the dig from the center of the river out to either shore. The finished tunnel is the closest most people ever get to U Thant Island: the 7 train passes through it directly underneath. When the shaft was filled in, the island was forgotten by all but cormorants, which nest there. In 1977 a UN group called the Peace Meditation at the United Nations leased the hump from the city, planted shrubs, and named it after the Burmese former Secretary General. For years, the only people allowed to set foot here was this group of UN employees.

Now it's totally off limits. Probably the most curious event in the island's history turns on this point. In the summer of 2004, during the Republican National Convention, local artist Duke Riley rowed out to U Thant in the early morning dark. He then hoisted a banner bearing a personal emblem of electric eels and claimed the island a sovereign nation. "I'm drawn to those environments," Riley says of New York's islands. "You're in one of the most hyper-developed cities in the world, and here are these tiny untouched secret places." While the Coast Guard was chasing him, they failed to notice Riley's banner, which flew from the navigation tower for days. When asked what he planned to call his miniature island nation, the artist pauses, then laughs. "Really, I don't even know if I got that far."

UPPER WEST SIDE
WEST SIDE
CENTRAL PARK
Hudson River
Park Riverside
Henry Hudson Parkway
Riverside Drive
Riverside Boulevard
Freedom Place
Dimaggio Highway
West End Ave.
Broadway
Amsterdam Ave.
Columbus Ave.
Manhattan Ave.
Central Park West
103 Street
96 Street
86 Street
79 Street
72 Street
66 Street-Lincoln Center
81 Street-Museum of Natural History
American Museum of Natural History
Lincoln Towers
Lincoln Center
The Pool
97th St. Transverse
86th St. Transverse
65th St. Transverse
The Lake
Strawberry Fields
The Sheep Meadow
Baseball Fields
0
200
400 m
N
1
2
3
4
5
6

UPPER WEST SIDE (59TH – 110TH)

01.

1 and 2 trains/66 Street – Lincoln Center
1, A, C, B and D trains/59 Street – Columbus Circle

33 WEST 63RD STREET

A stranded tenement

On the Upper West Side, at the bottom of a canyon of glass and brick residential towers, one small building stands out – or more accurately, has forced neighboring giants to stand awkwardly around it. 33 West 63rd Street is just five stories tall, bordered in rough-cut stone, with the full complement of black iron fire escapes zigzagging across the face. A tenement, in other words. It used to be one in a row – the walls on either side are windowless where adjacent buildings were shorn off – and the row used to be one in a large crop of tenements that sprang up in this neighborhood in the late 1800s and gradually broadened with the arrival of the IRT subway line in 1904.

How did No. 33 become so isolated? Spite, mostly. The owner, Jehiel R. Elyachar, was described by a former tenant of the lonely tenement as "a tiny, skinny, bent over little gnome of a man." He had made so much money in real estate and construction – a fortune of over $100 million, by one reckoning – he could indulge in the rich curmudgeon's preferred sport: mad stinginess. While giving generously to various Jewish-American and Israeli causes before he died in 1989, including schools and homes for the aged, Elyachar was the kind of guy who ends up getting sued by his own children. When developer Paul Milstein began buying several properties on the corner of Broadway and 63rd to build a retail and apartment tower, Elyachar agreed on a price, and then played out a series of bait-and-switch deals that were so fiendish, Milstein gradually understood that he was caught not in a business fiasco but some kind of sinister game. He finally threw up his hands and built his tower with an L-shaped footprint, leaving the stranded tenement where it was. And still is.

SAN JUAN HILL

Buildings come and go on a practically daily basis in New York, but to the west of the lonely tenement you can find the site where an entire neighborhood was swept from the map. The Upper West Side between 65th and 59th Streets at Amsterdam Avenue was once one of New York's largest African-American communities. Called San Juan Hill, a 1940 Housing Authority report deemed it "the worst slum in New York City." 1,500 families were displaced when the tenements were torn down to build the Lincoln Center, but demolition was delayed to film the gritty street scenes of West Side Story.

02.

135 West 70th Street
1, 2 and 3 trains/72nd Street

THE PYTHIAN

The fantastical lodge of a forgotten order

The inscription above the entrance to The Pythian reads: "If fraternal love held all men bound, how beautiful this world would be." The message is hard to argue with; what deadpan pharaohs and the monsters of Babylon have to do with it is open to question. This weird building is the work of architect Thomas W. Lamb, who made his name designing outrageous movie palaces in the 1920s (see page 236). He brought the same anything-goes attitude to The Pythian, looting along the way a hodgepodge of antiquity: snarling griffins, bull teams bearing gigantic urns, double-headed capitals and gilt hieroglyphs. Constructed in 1926, the building served as the central meeting place for New York's lodges of the Knights of Pythias.

Mostly unknown today, the Knights of Pythias was the first American fraternal organization chartered by an Act of Congress. Promoting charity and "universal peace," the Knights can boast three U.S. Presidents, including FDR, and at the time of The Pythian's construction fraternity was booming: over 100 lodges in New York City alone. The order's founder was inspired by the Greek legend of ancient travelers Damon and Pythias. Pythias was sentenced to death by the tyrant of Syracuse; Damon gallantly agreed to stand in for his friend while the latter went home to put his affairs in order, with the understanding that if Pythias skipped, Damon would be executed in his place. Panting Pythias showed up just as the axe was about to fall, and the tyrant was so impressed he freed both men. The two have symbolized selfless friendship ever since.

The Pythian is decorated with some of the strangest and most striking colored terracotta in the city, but you can scarcely find a New Yorker who knows it. Long gone is a chance to visit the polished stone lobby, the theater, or any one of the several lodge halls: The Pythian was chopped into condominiums in 1983. Asked if such a bizarre structure attracts bizarre residents, the doorman shakes his head. "Nice people," he says. "Normal people. If I could afford it, I'd live here." At last check, a one-bedroom runs about $1 million.

Although they're gone from this address, the Knights still exist: there areover 2,000 lodges worldwide.

When membership in the order fell off, the Knights of Pythias leased part of the building to Decca Records, where in 1954 Bill Haley and His Comets recorded their Top 40 juggernaut "Rock Around the Clock".

IF FRATERNAL LOVE
HELD ALL MEN BOUND
HOW BEAUTIFUL
THIS WORLD WOULD
The Pythian

03.

256 West 71st Street
nycgovparks.org/parks/M282
1, 2 and 3 trains/72nd Street

SEPTUAGESIMO UNO PARK

The smallest park in the five boroughs

Central Park is Manhattan's largest park, of course. To give some idea of the vastness, just a dozen years ago researchers discovered buried under the leaves a genus of centipede totally unknown to science. If your taste in green goes in a cozier direction, head three blocks west on 71st Street to Septuagesimo Uno. It takes less time to walk past this park than pronounce the name (it means "seventy-one"). At 0.04 acres it's New York City's smallest.

The story of this curious nook cuts right to the core of Manhattan urban planning. At a time when uptown was still dotted with farmhouses, Mayor DeWitt Clinton implemented his far-sighted Commissioners' Plan of 1811, dividing the island above 14th Street into the grid system of north-south avenues and east-west cross streets we take for granted today. Although public parks were figured in (at 53rd, 66th, 77th, and 120th Streets), by the 1960s the growing population and crush of buildings had outpaced the average New Yorker's ability not to go insane.

This situation was eased somewhat by Mayor John Lindsay's Vest Pocket park initiative. Since everywhere was already crammed with buildings, the initiative specialized in sprucing up the vacant lots between them. Septuagesimo Uno is just brownstone-width. It may be the only park in New York City with a street address: 256 West 71st Street – the address of a house that was condemned in 1969 and whose narrow footprint the park now occupies. The City of New York Parks & Recreation signs block most of the view when the gates are closed, and the standard list of prohibitions becomes comedy: "Performing or rallying, except by permit" (where?); "Obstructing entrances to the park" (there's only one, and if you're reading the sign, you're obstructing). With its wooden benches, slender plant beds, and single tree, what Septuagesimo Uno is big enough for is you and a friend, or just you and a book. It may be all you need.

04.

368 West End Avenue
westendchurch.org
1 and 2 trains/79th Street

MILLSTONES OF THE COLLEGIATE REFORMED PROTESTANT DUTCH CHURCH

The oldest pieces of colonial New York

On West End Avenue at 77th Street there's a brick Flemish-style church. Inside, at the entrance to the main chapel, are stacked three large circular stones girt in iron with holes in the middle. They look like they would be more comfortable in a barn, but for history they're unbeatable. The stones are millstones, and they're likely the oldest pieces we have of colonial New York.

The West End Collegiate does little to publicize the stones because as an institution it has very little to prove. Established by British royal charter in 1696, the church is the single oldest corporation in the United States. But the millstones aren't just part of an eccentric collection of old colonial hardware: they speak to the very essence of the early church. Dutch settlers came to New York (they called it New Amsterdam) in 1624. There is a record, just two years later, of a François Molemaecker "employed in building a horse-mill, with spacious room above, to serve for a congregation." The location of this mill became Mill Lane; there's still a block-long snippet of it left between Stone and William Streets. Amused American Indians used to come to service and fill the loft with pipe smoke while they laughed, as if to deliberately goad fussy Jonas Michaelius, the pastor. "As to the natives of this country," he wrote, "I find them entirely savage and wild, strangers to all decency, yea, uncivil and stupid as garden poles, proficient in all wickedness and godlessness." But like all earlier chroniclers, he is awestruck by the beauty and natural abundance of primeval Manhattan.

The millstones are actually older than New York – or any other American city. They were quarried in Belgium and brought here with the earliest settlers. The church met at the mill until 1633, when it moved to a plain building on Broad Street (now long gone). The mill address was taken over by Shearith Israel, New York's earliest Jewish congregation.

When Shearith Israel moved uptown to 70th Street, they dug up the old stones, kept two (you can see them in the synagogue), and gave four to the Collegiate Church. One is now embedded in the alley wall of next-door Collegiate School. Three stayed in the church narthex.

05.

Riverside Drive at 93rd Street
1, 2 and 3 trains/96th Street

JOAN OF ARC ISLAND

Stones from Joan's prison tower in Rouen, and fragments from the cathedral at Reims

There is indeed a place in New York City with the winsome name "Joan of Arc Island." But far from a wooded sanctuary where teenage girls with swords roam free, it's an island only in the sense of traffic island – that is, an enclosed urban area bordered by a curb. The main event is an equestrian statue at the center, lined up directly with 93rd Street. Saint Joan, staring straight into the sky.

There are plenty of women in New York City statues but they're mostly mythological or allegorical: the Joan of Arc was the first based on an actual woman. It's also the city's only statue – and wherever there are statues of Joan of Arc this tends to be true – of a woman seated on a horse. The artist, Anna Hyatt Huntington, was the daughter of a professor of zoology and an accomplished animal artist who, after moving to Paris to refine her technique, became captivated by the maiden warrior. Determined to create a work honoring Joan's consecration, Huntington visited the French sites associated with key events in her personal history. At that time in Reims there was a Paul DuBois statue of Joan of Arc (and a copy of it in Paris) that closely resembles Huntington's in having the gaze fixed on the sky, but the American sculptor puts the heaviest emphasis on the sword. "When [Joan] went into battle," Huntington said, "she unconsciously raised it to heaven to ask the blessing of the Lord on it...That was the idea of the statue."

In 1910, Huntington submitted a life-size plaster model of Joan to the Paris Salon, where it received honorable mention and some sexist amazement. More important, the work completely won over members of a New York monument committee dedicated to commemorating the 500th anniversary of the saint's birth. The statue was unveiled on 93rd Street three years late (1915), but the lag provided a detail that makes this work truly unique. The base includes stones from a tower in Rouen where Joan was imprisoned, and fragments from the cathedral at Reims where, thanks to her, Charles VII was crowned. Stone from France's great historical buildings was depressingly available in 1915: the Germans had started bombing a year earlier.

OTHER FRAGMENTS OF THE BOMBED REIMS CATHEDRAL

Corpus Christi Church on West 121st Street and Broadway also has fragments of the bombed Reims Cathedral: stained glass in the apse windows.

06.

319 West 107th Street
roerich.org
1 train/110th Street

NICHOLAS ROERICH MUSEUM

Townhouse for a mystic

The brownstone at 319 West 107th is a three-story tribute to the mystical Russian painter Nicholas Roerich. At the door there's a modest plaque and a bell. When you enter, there might be no one in the vestibule to meet you. You might hear someone practicing on the piano on the second floor, or pass a silent visitor on the wooden stair – but most likely, you'll have the house to yourself.

Intimacy is the special feature of this small museum, following the motto of the late director Daniel Entin ("Do whatever you want. Spend as long as you like."). Entin was an unassuming white-bearded gentleman with a gleam in his eye that hinted at hidden resources. He used to live on the ground floor of the museum he had directed for three decades. If you wanted to chat, he would sit you at the kitchen table and tell you what he knew about Nicholas Roerich, which was pretty much everything. What you wouldn't hear: why you came in the first place. "Roerich's painting is just the kind of art that touches a certain kind of person," Entin would say. "There's something that grabs the people whom it grabs. Others couldn't care less." The director seemed okay with either type.

There are over 200 Roerich works here, but his greatness as a painter is beside the point: the museum is less art collection than spiritual center. Nicholas Roerich became interested in Eastern philosophy in 1910, when he helped design the first-ever Tibetan temple outside Asia in St. Petersburg. His life thereafter was structured by two overlapping interests: Buddhism, and the unity of mankind through the arts. He'd already gathered a following in Russia when the Revolution forced him to move to the States; after outgrowing several buildings, he had a large complex erected on the corner of Riverside and West 103rd, with schools for every branch of the arts, teacher and student residences, and exhibition spaces. The building is still there, but the school didn't survive the Depression. Shortly after the painter's death in 1947, the Nicholas Roerich Museum was founded on nearby West 107th Street.

The paintings, vividly colored allegories and landscapes reflecting Roerich's expeditions in Tibet, cover the walls of the elegant brownstone. Admirers come from distant countries, seeking a spiritual connection, but Entin was most touched by the walk-ins. "A lot of them are in and out in 3 minutes. Then somebody will come in and burst into tears."

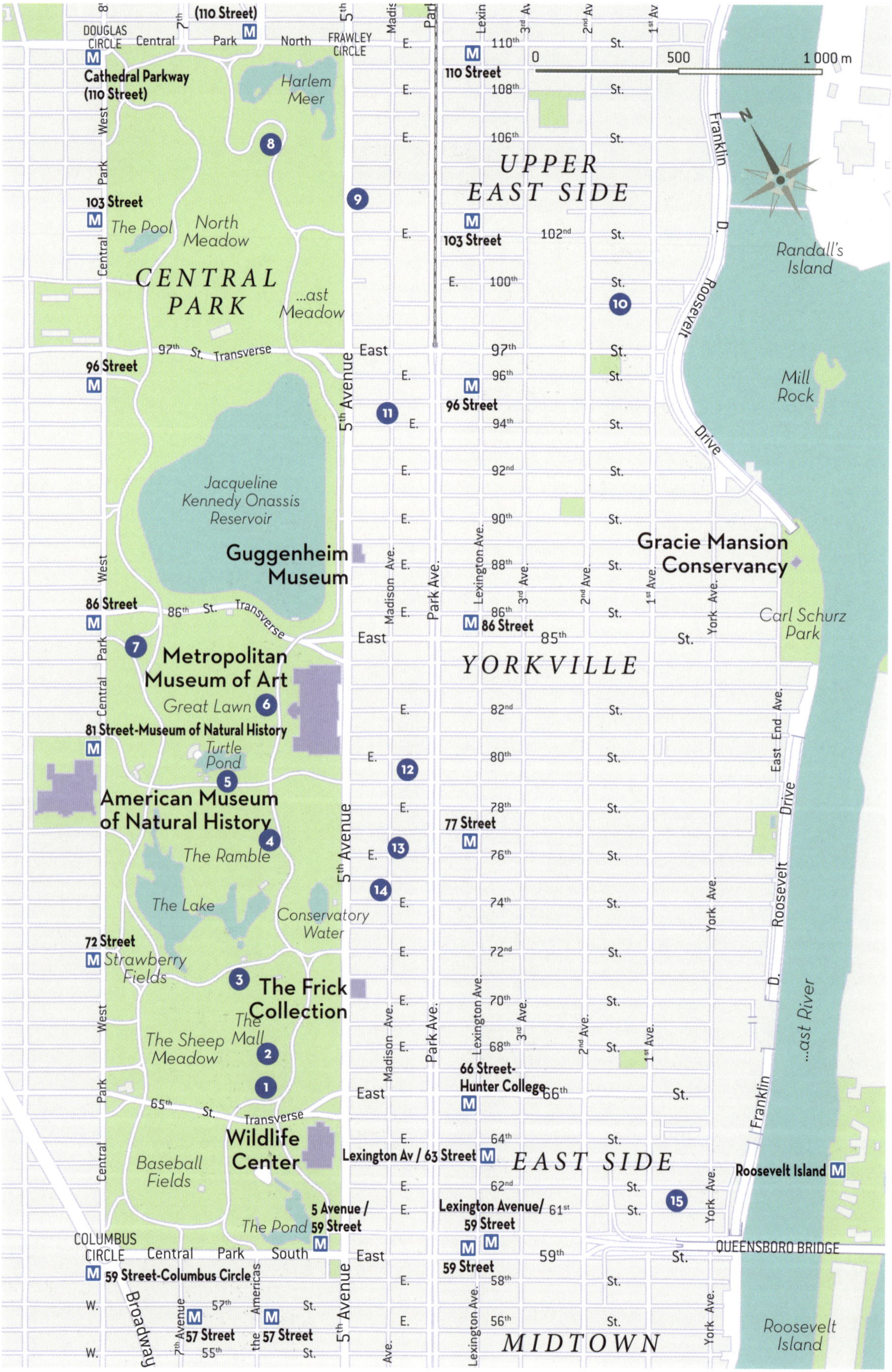
UPPER EAST SIDE
CENTRAL PARK
YORKVILLE
EAST SIDE
MIDTOWN
Harlem Meer
The Pool
North Meadow
Jacqueline Kennedy Onassis Reservoir
Guggenheim Museum
Metropolitan Museum of Art
Great Lawn
Turtle Pond
American Museum of Natural History
The Ramble
The Lake
Conservatory Water
Strawberry Fields
The Frick Collection
The Sheep Meadow
The Mall
Wildlife Center
Baseball Fields
The Pond
Gracie Mansion Conservancy
Carl Schurz Park
Randall's Island
Mill Rock
Roosevelt Island
QUEENSBORO BRIDGE
DOUGLAS CIRCLE
FRAWLEY CIRCLE
COLUMBUS CIRCLE
Central Park North
Central Park South
Central Park West
97th St. Transverse
86th St. Transverse
65th St. Transverse
5th Avenue
Madison Ave.
Park Ave.
Lexington Ave.
3rd Ave.
2nd Ave.
1st Ave.
York Ave.
East End Ave.
Franklin D. Roosevelt Drive
Broadway
Cathedral Parkway (110 Street)
(110 Street)
103 Street
96 Street
86 Street
81 Street-Museum of Natural History
72 Street
59 Street-Columbus Circle
57 Street
110 Street
77 Street
66 Street-Hunter College
Lexington Av / 63 Street
5 Avenue / 59 Street
Lexington Avenue/ 59 Street
59 Street
Roosevelt Island
0
500
1 000 m
N

UPPER EAST SIDE AND CENTRAL PARK

01.

Central Park
Shakespeare is located at the head of the Mall
(where East Drive connects with Center Drive at about 66th Street),
Indian Hunter 100 yards west (toward Sheep Meadow)

PHRENOLOGY IN CENTRAL PARK

Highbrow, lowbrow: Shakespeare vs. the American Indian

Two statues at the entrance to the Central Park Mall – Shakespeare, and an American Indian – offer a tidy illustration of one of history's more harebrained notions. Phrenology, the "science" of determining character and personality traits by the shape of the skull, was a hot ticket in New York in the mid-19th century. Two enterprising quacks, the Fowler brothers, got rich off the idea at their Nassau Street office, where they made consultations, gave lectures, and published books and journals. Edgar Allan Poe was a devotee, as was Walt Whitman (perhaps because the Fowlers told him his bumpy skull indicated "a tendency to the pleasures of voluptuousness"). The most influential New Yorker of the time, William Cullen Bryant, had such respect for phrenology he made it central to a speech he gave in the spring of 1872 to celebrate the unveiling of the John Quincy Adams Ward statue of Shakespeare.

"Come down to the phrenologists of the present day," Bryant said as the crowd admired the new bronze, "and they tell you of the visible indications of his boundless invention, his universal sympathy, his lofty idealism, his wit, his humor..." Bryant, the namesake of Bryant Park, was a poet, editor, publisher, and general advocate of public welfare. That this decent, educated man also believed that Shakespeare's genius was written wholesale in his "noble countenance" shows how entrenched the pseudoscience was.

While Bryant was delivering his speech, another statue – by the same sculptor, no less – crouched stealthily only a hundred paces to the west. Ward's Indian Hunter was modeled on sketches the artist made in the Dakotas, and praised as a true model of "aboriginal physiogonomical types." The difference to Shakespeare's smooth, egg-like head couldn't be starker. The American Indian's hairline starts so low, it looks like he's wearing some sort of bushy headgear.

Today we're less likely to scrutinize foreheads for signs of talent, but the stain of pseudoscience persists in the language. If you consider these two statues, you are witnessing the origins of the term "high brow," meaning sophisticated, and "low brow," meaning the opposite. It's the legacy of yesterday's crackpot fad.

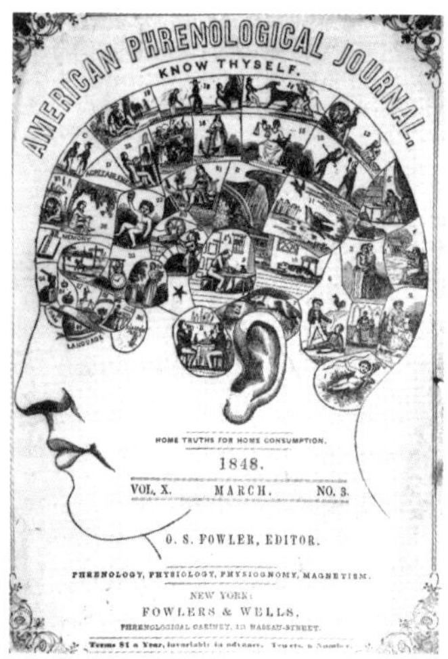

02.

Central Park
The Mall (beginning where East Drive connects with Center Drive at about 66th Street, ending at Bethesda Terrace)

THE ELM TREES OF CENTRAL PARK

The best-tended trees in the world

Central Park has over 25,000 individual trees, of about 150 different species. Those that line the Mall – the wide, straight path that leads to Bethesda Terrace – are American elms (*Ulmus americana*). The tunnel of foliage they create is one of the favorite images of New York, and seems as fixed as the Empire State Building or the Brooklyn Bridge. But these elms require constant, fretful attention: a pall of death hangs over them, and always has.

The Mall was intended to be Central Park's answer to the allées of France's geometric gardens. The straighaway is the exception in park designers Frederick Law Olmsted and Calvert Vaux's plan, otherwise based on interwoven loops and curves. The preference for the Mall's trees was from the very beginning the American elm – the choice, according to the Parks Department, of "almost every Main Street and college campus in the country in the 19th century." The soil was judged unfit for the large transplants; the contractor, in a gesture that resonates like an omen today, vowed that if the trees failed to survive for three years he would forfeit his fee. A year later nearly all of them were dead. A second group of smaller trees followed, and survived into the early 1900s – when gradually they, too, began to die.

Most of the elms we see in the Mall today date from around 1920. At the same time a biologist in Holland identified a fungus, spread by beetles, that came to be called Dutch elm disease. It soon crossed the Atlantic, and began to ravage the shade trees on those countless Main Streets and campuses. Most of New York's American elms have died; many consider those on the Central Park Mall to be the greatest collection anywhere.

Nobody feels the weight of this more than Neil Calvanese, Operations Vice-President of the Central Park Conservancy. "Beetles you can deal with," he says. "Fungus you can deal with. But fungus carried by beetles? It's an elm-killing machine." When the Conservancy started managing the park in 1998, the elms became a special priority. They are scrutinized for any sign of the disease, branches are fastidiously tested, whole trees are uprooted to prevent spreading. Calvanese figures the cost of protecting the elms has amounted to "millions of dollars." They may be the best-tended trees in the world.

03.

Central Park
Located at the top of Bethesda Terrace
at the head of the central stair

THE WITCH OF BETHESDA TERRACE

The life of the night

The larger impact of Bethesda – fountain, lake, boats, forest – is so visually gratifying, it's perhaps natural that the fine details go unnoticed. The stone of the entire terrace is textured with sculptures, each unique, comprising what Central Park's first critics judged the richest public carving in America. The work is abstract in places, and figurative in others, and often a skillful collision of the two. The weirdest detail is the wicked tableau on one of the two large stone posts at the top of the stair passage: a flying witch, a jack-o'-lantern, a crescent moon.

The designer of the stonework was Jacob Wrey Mould, an English immigrant and something of a mad wizard. In 1868, when the park was nearly finished, the British magazine The Builder called him "brilliant, accomplished, ingenious, erratic." This sounds like a fair description of someone who, after designing the eye-watering arabesques and teeming birds lower down the terrace, would top it off with a witch. There's a calculated method at work, however. "He has delight in his art," cooed Clarence Cook in one of the first descriptions of the park, "that it is far easier for him to make every fresh design an entirely new one, than to copy something he has made before." Examine the pendant motifs of the posts and the medallions on the balustrade and you'll see what Cook meant. The interwoven patterns are an effect that Mould picked up from Islamic design, of which he was an expert; the balustrades, with their swirling birds and plants, represent the four seasons. Up above, on the other side of the carriage path (renamed Olmsted & Vaux Way after the park's designers) you'll find two stone posts: the witch flies on the western face of the western one.

West because: it's the direction of the setting sun. The carved scenes represent the different times of day: the witch's thematic opposite (eastern face of the eastern post) features a sunrise over the ocean. It's been suggested that the witch and the jack-o'-lantern, as symbols of Halloween, were Mould's way of either slighting or honoring the Irish, who brought the tradition to the city. But it's as likely that he was simply having clever fun. How to express the dead of night, a time that is effectively invisible? D.H. Lawrence said that birds are the life of the skies; well, the witch is the life of the night.

04.

Central Park
In the Ramble at about 76th Street;
walk uphill on East Drive from Loeb Boathouse,
turn left at the bronze panther and go 50 paces due west

KENTUCKY COFFEE TREES

Mastodon food in Central Park

There is a small stand of very odd trees in Central Park. They're highly poisonous: even insects stay away. Tough seed pods hang uneaten on the bare branches far into winter. The fallen seeds are ignored by pretty much every living thing except paleontologists. For instance Carl Mehling of the American Museum of Natural History: "I mean, what would bother with this?" he asks, plucking what looks like a blob of dark glass from the soil. He knows the answer: a mastodon.

Seed dispersal is a vital trick in every plant's adaptive skill set. Some seeds fly on fibrous wings, some exploit the forgetfulness of hoarding squirrels, many are happiest in manure. In a 1982 paper, biologist Daniel Janzen and geoscientist Paul Martin addressed an ecological puzzle: why the fruits of some trees rot untouched, and why their husk is too tough or seeds too big for critters to eat. It was thought that plants with ineffectual "dispersal syndromes" were poorly evolved; Janzen and Martin suggested that they are in fact beautifully, exquisitely evolved, but the creatures they were tailored to attract – mastodons, giant sloths – went extinct 12,000 years ago.

A book on the theory, "The Ghosts of Evolution" (Connie Barlow), places the Kentucky coffee tree in the tiny category of "extreme anachronisms" – plants that make little sense in their present ecology. Since the end of the Pleistocene they've relied on floods and chance to keep the species going; meanwhile they're haunted by what once ate them. In the grass Mehling spies a fallen pod and cracks it open. Inside, seeds glisten in energy-rich goop like green rubber cement. "So good," he says, breathing deep. "Like chocolate and bananas." Now you know what mastodons like. To make the glassy seeds germinate, Mehling explains that you have to "scar" them, as the teeth and gastric juices of gobbling Pleistocene megafauna would. Otherwise they'll remain marbles forever.

But just because decorative mastodon food grows in Central Park doesn't mean that the beasts really lived on Manhattan? "Corner of Broadway and Dyckman," Mehling says back in the museum's fossil room; he points at a brown lower jawbone the size of a dinner platter. Fossils from a dozen mastodons have turned up in New York City, two of them in Manhattan. "Look at those teeth," Mehling nods. Each one is deeply ridged, and bigger than your fist.

05.

Central Park
79th Street Transverse, midway at Belvedere Castle

ROCK TUNNEL TRANSVERSE

Fresh eyes on a marvel

Much has been made of Central Park's illusory "naturalness." One aspect of this feat of planning is seldom remarked today: the flow of foot and vehicle (and horse) traffic within and through the park. How to work an 840-acre block of green into the guts of a growing metropolis? It was a problem, and the area at Belvedere Castle, a schist outcrop called Vista Rock, was a particularly sticky part of it. Central Park designers Frederick Law Olmsted and Calvert Vaux likely owed the success of their proposal to striking on an inspired solution: sinking transverses below ground level. You can walk the whole length of the park (recommended) and never realize that major city arteries flow under your feet. The first visitors in the 1860s were amazed by the multi-level character of the paths and transverses: the experience of seeing cross-traffic in any form passing directly below or directly above was totally novel.

Today our experience with cars, and the freeways and onramps of major cities, make multi-level traffic seem mundane. But there's one spot in the park where you can witness this engineering challenge of the 1850s with fresh eyes. The footpath down Vista Rock branches off to the right about 50 yards east of the castle, leading seemingly nowhere. Take it. Go down the stone stairs. Emerge onto the 79th Street transverse, with more or less constant east-west car and bus traffic. Olmsted and Vaux foresaw this congestion, but imagined the transverse choked with "coal carts and butcher's carts, dust carts and dung carts." Believe it or not, standing here below the promontory to appreciate the tunnel blasted through the schist was a favorite thing for early park visitors to do. In 1869 Clarence Cook described the tunnel with a lingering distrust in its newfangledness. "After careful examination," he wrote, "the roof was found to be sound and firm." Going to see the blasted rock was so popular, this nice stone staircase was added some years after the park's completion.

The tunnel was created with gunpowder. Dynamite hadn't been invented yet.

12'-0"
11'-0"

06.

Central Park
On the west side of East Drive at about 83rd Street, behind the Metropolitan Museum of Art
nycgovparks.org/parks/centralpark/highlights/11942

GRANITE STATUE OF ALEXANDER HAMILTON

A reminder of the Great Fire

Fires have always been a mortal threat to New York, and especially so before the city installed its first major water distribution system in 1842 (see page 50). There are no monuments to the great blazes of the past, only absences. The last traces of the Dutch period were erased from downtown in successive fires in the 19th century, and one disaster, the so-called Great Fire of 1835, destroyed more property than any other event in the city's history. The statue of Alexander Hamilton that stands in Central Park, while not exactly a fire memorial, is a curious reminder.

The Great Fire began with a gas explosion in a dry goods store on today's Beaver Street. It was a frigid December night: roaring winds soon spread the flames to the surrounding buildings while bucket brigades and volunteer firemen tried to chip through the iced-over wells to water, which then froze in the hoses or blew back in sprays of cutting ice. The blaze soon spread to the Merchants' Exchange on Wall Street. Inside was the first marble work ever carved in the United States: a 14-foot-tall Alexander Hamilton by sculptor Robert Ball Hughes. The monument, celebrated as the country's finest statue, depicted Hamilton in classical robes and stood tall in the Exchange's Grand Rotunda. Dodging flames, a group of sailors dashed in to save the statue; they managed to lift it from the base and were wrestling it toward the exit when the roof collapsed and they fled for their lives. According to a later account: "The artist stood gazing on the scene with listless despair; and when his favourite production of his genius, on which he had bestowed the labour of two long years fell beneath the ruins he sobbed and wept like a child."

A model of the work can be found at the Museum of the City of New York. The statue standing today in Central Park, by Carl Conrad, was commissioned by Alexander Hamilton's youngest son John Church Hamilton. It's carved from a material you don't see in many portrait statues: granite. John Church is said to have chosen the durable stone so that whatever future disaster the city had in store, this time his father's monument would survive.

HAMILTON

07.

Central Park
Footprint of the village was between 81st and 89th Streets and between old Seventh and Eighth Avenues; foundation stones are 50 yards east of the children's playground at the 85th Street entrance

SENECA

A vanished village

In a page from the Times dated July 9, 1856, we learn the following: John Humphries was arrested for assault (two stabs with a sheath-knife); a new fire engine was given a trial run on Franklin Street; Mr. George Armstrong drowned on a fishing excursion; and by the end of the month, a whole community would have to vacate the area west of the old reservoir. "Within the limits of the Central Park," reads the article, "lies a neat little settlement [...] It is to be hoped that their removal will be effected with as much gentleness as possible."

The village had a proper name: Seneca. There's only one physical trace of it left, the corner of a stone foundation at about 85th Street across the path from the children's playground.

By all accounts, Seneca was exceptional. Even the Times article is careful to note the "pleasing contrast" it made to the miserable shanties of the Irish ("in common with hogs and goats") further south. Founded in 1825, the village had three churches, wood houses on assigned lots, a natural spring, basement schools, and a population of over 260, mostly African American. Far from a ghetto, it was a rural refuge from the chaos, disease, and bigotry of downtown. It also gave Black residents what they needed by law in order to vote: their own land.

In 1853, the city passed a bill authorizing the takeover of the swath of Manhattan destined to become Central Park. Seneca plot owners were paid off and the settlement was erased. In the summer of 2011, a team of Columbia archeologists dug in the area and found the minutiae of village life: crockery, cooking pans, a child's shoe.

Ashley Anderson, an educator who assisted with the digs, found a belt buckle. "There were other primarily African American villages," she says, "but a progressive community, and middle class? It was monumental." She also reveals a detail that is not covered in the Conservancy tour: the corner of foundation, supposedly the only physical trace of Seneca, is not that of a church, as was generally believed, but actually a later construction built exactly on top of it.

In other words all that's left of Seneca is a kind of architectural echo, and what still lies hidden underground. When asked where these pioneering African Americans went, Anderson only shakes her head. No one has been able to find out.

08.

Central Park
After turning onto Central Park Driveway (at about 104th Street) from East Drive, take the first northbound path and continue about 60 yards
nycgovparks.org/parks/central-park/monuments/638

ANDREW HASWELL GREEN MEMORIAL BENCH

The father of greater New York

On January 1, 1898, New Yorkers woke up to a city that had nearly doubled in size from the previous day to 3.5 million, making it the second largest in the world after London. The reason was the consolidation of the boroughs – Manhattan, Bronx, Queens, Brooklyn, and Staten Island – and the man behind the plan was one Andrew Haswell Green. In the far north of Central Park, at the edge of a small clearing on top of a hill, there is a large marble bench. It's the only monument to Green in New York City.

Creating the metropolis boundaries earned Green the nickname "Father of Greater New York" and is more than enough reason to memorialize him. But the man's influence goes further. In 1895, generations before the city would finally confront its own self-destructive forces in the 1960s, Green founded the American Scenic and Historic Preservation Society, dedicated to protecting city green spaces. He served on the Board of Commissioners during Central Park's construction, and is largely responsible for keeping the plans in line with the masterpiece that designers Frederick Law Olmsted and Calvert Vaux originally conceived. Green was also crucial to the formation of the New York Public Library, which without him would have had no book circulation.

And here's this marble bench. It's in the unvisited northern end of the park, and accessed by a narrow trail that even those who know the place are lucky to find twice. In the summer the grass is yellow; in winter the snow goes unshoveled. There is litter all around. A roomy, smooth stone bench in a secluded spot surrounded by trees: it might as well have a sign that says "Vagrants Welcome".

If you think Green deserved better, how the man is remembered is rather sweet compared to how he died. "Andrew H. Green Murdered," reads the Times headline from November 14, 1903. A man named Cornelius Williams stalked Green as he was returning from work and, just as the 83-year-old approached the iron gate of his home on 40th Street, shot him five times with a pistol. "He deserved it!" Williams stated in testimony. "He forced me to do it!" It later turned out that not only was Green innocent of any wrongdoing, he and his killer had never even met.

1820 IN HONOR OF ANDREW HASWELL GREEN
DIRECTING GENIUS OF CENTRAL PARK IN ITS FORMATIVE PERIOD
FATHER OF GREATER NEW YORK THIS EMINENCE WAS NAMED ANDREW H GREEN HILL
THESE FIVE SYMBOLICAL TREES WERE PLANTED AND THIS SEAT WAS ERECTED

09.

Museum of the City of New York
1220 Fifth Avenue
mcny.org
4 and 6 trains/103rd Street

PAINTINGS IN THE STETTHEIMER DOLLHOUSE

A small but distinguished collection

A rare version of Marcel Duchamp's "Nude Descending a Staircase" hangs in the Stettheimer ballroom. Drawn in ink, wash, and graphite, and signed by Duchamp on the lower left, the work captures all the energy and daring of one of modernism's great masterpieces. To get the full benefit, enter the ballroom through the north door and then work gradually right. Also, be five inches tall.

The painting is one of many you'll find in New York's most improbable art collection, the Stettheimer dollhouse, where the paintings and drawings, generally not much bigger than postage stamps, are not facsimiles but *real* – bona fide works of art from the hand of celebrated artists. The Stettheimers – Carrie, who made the dollhouse, and her sisters Ettie and Florine – were daughters of a wealthy German banker who deserted them when they were children. After years touring Europe, the sisters and their mother settled in New York at the ritzy Alwyn Court on West 58th Street. The Stettheimers were defiantly "modern": they smoked cigarettes, rejected romance, marriage, and children, and had a theatrical penchant for bright wigs, diamond collars, and Venetian costumes. Their apartment became a popular salon among the artists and intellectuals of New York's avant-garde. Florine, a painter, was the driving force; Ettie, a writer, was the wit and conversationalist; Carrie was the hostess and miniaturist. She was nearly 50 when she began the dollhouse, fashioning many of the finely detailed furnishings by hand. The tiny paintings were presented by artists who frequented the salon; the ballroom contains works by renowned modernists Duchamp, Albert Gleizes, and Alexander Archipenko, among others, as well as a pair of drawings and a six-inch alabaster statue by Gaston Lachaise.

Ettie offered the dollhouse to the museum after Carrie's death in 1945. Florine Stettheimer surmised that Carrie doted on the house (30 years in all) as a way of sublimating a frustrated ambition to be a set designer. The reader might surmise that the Stettheimer's bohemian salon was a collective sublimation of three women trapped in a kind of permanent childhood. Whatever the case, "Nude Descending a Staircase" alone is worth a visit.

10.

343 East 99th Street
6 train/96 Street

GARBAGE MUSEUM

Why would somebody throw that away?

That Billy Joel's Greatest Hits album you threw away in 1995, for a perfectly good reason, exists somewhere. It might be floating in the ocean, or under 40 feet of rot in a landfill, or ash on the wind. Or, if it's lucky, sitting in a clean crate with other undesirables in a Sanitation Department depot on East 99th Street as one of thousands of "exhibits" in the Garbage Museum.

The museum isn't in any way official, and you won't find it in any guide to the city. What it offers isn't even really intended for your amusement. It's a vast collection of objects that, for whatever reason, prompted a trash collector on his rounds to pause and ask the question: Why would somebody throw that away? Sanitation workers are the ultimate arbiters of value in New York City, and from time to time they grant reprieves. As powers go, this one is pretty great. Unloved toys, frumpy technology, posters in cheap frames, paintings by artists with no discernible talent, silent cuckoo clocks, second-place bowling trophies. Many of the objects fall into the flexible "perfectly good" category: old books and albums, kitchenware and sports equipment. Others are freakish riddles: a real dog, enormous, muscled, stuffed like a hunter's memento.

As with most great things, the Garbage Museum owes its existence to the quirks of one man. Nelson Molina first started bringing in objects off the street in 1981 to decorate his own area of the locker room. Slowly, the exhibit expanded as co-workers added their own rescued items. "It doesn't matter what it is," Molina told the Times. "As long as it's cool, I can hang it up and I've got a place for it."

What the Garbage Museum makes a place for isn't what you would choose to make a place for, and this is the better part of what's good about it. While you probably won't be chased out ("It's not for me to tell you where you can go and can't go," says one worker on the sidewalk out front), you won't be pandered to. These guys have made a display of our collective sense of value. It's about us, but not for us.

34

11.

Madison Avenue between 94th and 95th Streets
4 and 6 trains/96th Street

SQUADRON A ARMORY

The castle on Madison Avenue

First-time visitors to the Upper East Side are often pleased to discover that there's what appears to be an entire medieval castle on Madison Avenue. Two towers of red brick look down on the street, with arrow slits and turrets, and even crenellated tops. Today the walls enclose a school: look through, about where you'd expect the drawbridge to be, onto a playground full of yelling kids.

The castle was once home to Squadron A, the "New-York Hussars," an elite social club that used the yard inside for mounted drills. The building was started in 1894; the Hussars, originally strictly for show and sport, became a unit of the New York State National Guard in 1889 and went on to fight in the Spanish-American War and in both World Wars. On the wall you see a bronze plaque with their motto: *BOUTEZ EN AVANT* ("Charge").

The style of the brick building has been reported as "ancient Norman castellated," but it might as well be Camelot. Periodically, you can even see tendrils of ivy crawling up the rounded corners, as though arranged there by a fastidious backdrop artist. If you enjoy the incongruity of castles above taxicabs, you might appreciate it more to learn that the turrets, the towers and everything else were nearly knocked to rubble. When the Squadron A Armory became a school, plans were made to replace the towers with 16-story modernist replacements. But the city, still reeling from the destruction of Penn Station (see page 126) landmarked the building in 1966.

ISLAMIC CULTURAL CENTER

Three blocks to the east of the Squadron A Armory is an interesting case of a building that occupies the pitiless grid on its own terms. Most New York mosques interpret the direction of Mecca to be simply "east." But, as mentioned elsewhere (see pages 102, 130 and 164) Manhattan's grid is tilted to fit the island. The designers of the Islamic Cultural Center of New York at 1711 Third Avenue dispelled any doubt about the true direction of the holiest site in Islam by orienting their mosque to the exact geodesic – the shortest possible line between two points on a sphere – with Mecca. What looks crooked on the map is Islamically perfect.

12.

52 East 80th Street
4, 5 and 6 trains/77th Street or 86 Street

THE ZIEGFELD HEAD

The last piece of a legendary theater

Perhaps because we most associate statuary with antiquity, when buildings become unwanted it pains us to see the decoration tossed in the trash. New York has offered more of that kind of pain than most American cities. The landmarks conservation movement was in part sparked when a photographer discovered a stone angel from the recently demolished Penn Station (see page 126) leaning among rubble in a New Jersey dump. When the legendary Ziegfeld Theatre was sold a couple of years later and slated for razing, New Yorkers cried out but the newly-formed Landmarks Commission was powerless to stop the destruction. Today the Ziegfeld is dust, but one piece still survives. It sits on East 80th Street, behind a gate, near the basement entrance of a townhouse and – as if to make a point – next to the trashcans.

Designed by Viennese set designer and architect Joseph Urban, the Ziegfeld Theatre was created to be less a building than an otherworldly experience. "Unlike most of us, who see art in the flat terms of our environment," reads a Times article on the theater's 1927 opening, "Mr. Urban is a creator who paints nothing more tangible than dreams." Inside, the theater was shaped like an egg with the walls curving toward the stage; outside was a modernist proscenium arch in limestone with colossal engaged columns on either side, the fluting like the folds of a drawn curtain. Bright floodlights raked the white building at night, creating dodging patterns of shadow and glow on West 54th Street. High above the entrance perched stylized masks of comedy and tragedy, curved and ribbed like ram's horns; draped over them were 12-foot-tall protectoresses with mesmerizing eyes.

The Depression ruined the theater's Broadway business. After becoming a movie venue, and then a television studio, it finally folded in 1966 and was sold to make room for a soulless glass and steel tower. Shortly after the deal, theatrical producer Jerry Hammer was riding in a limousine with the property's developer. When they passed the old stone theater, the developer said he was about to demolish it; as a joke, Hammer said if that was the case he wanted one of the giant staring guardians. Four months later he heard noises outside his townhouse on East 80th Street. "It's a truck with a crane," Hammer told the Times, "and a head, and they ask me where I want it." The head has been here ever since.

52E80

13.

Carlyle Hotel
35 East 76th Street
thecarlyle.com
4 and 6 trains/77th Street

THE MURALS OF BEMELMANS BAR

Murals for rent

Bemelmans Bar in the Carlyle Hotel is mellow and warm, as if the whole room is encased in 1930s amber. The bar itself is polished granite bordered in leather, the tables are topped with black glass, the gold leaf ceiling casts powdery reflections. But eventually in the dim light you'll start to notice the walls – or the odd characters painted on them. A leggy kangaroo, for example, sitting at a café table with a joey in its pouch. A giraffe with pinstriped trousers and lace-up shoes (four of them), doffing its hat to a passer-by. A rabbit smoking a cigar. Since 1947, the bar has carried off a design triumph unique in New York City: the meeting of liquor and children's illustration.

The author of the paintings and bar namesake is Ludwig Bemelmans, an Austrian writer and artist who moved to New York while still in his teens. For years young Bemelmans was a busboy at the Ritz-Carlton Hotel; he used to hide behind the palm trees in the dining room and sketch people on the backs of menus. In 1939 he published the first in a series of books about a mischievous French girl named Madeline who lives in a Parisian boarding school. They made him famous.

"The mural," says Tommy the barman, nodding to the characters on the walls, "shows the four seasons in Central Park." Tommy has worked at the Carlyle for half a century and has the gift of rapid, respectful small talk. While he tells the story he squeaks out cork after cork from wine bottles without even looking down. "But it's the four seasons in Central Park with animals instead of people. And years ago." Certain landmarks you'll recognize: Belvedere Castle, Cleopatra's Needle. But these exist in an unhinged dimension where dachshunds wear Panama hats and bunnies build giant snowrabbits. Why it works is a pleasant riddle. Bemelmans' hand isn't cute: it's loose and classy at the same time, and makes its own kind of sense.

Bemelmans liked travel, and hotel life. Instead of taking money for the mural he opted for eighteen months rent-free at the Carlyle for him and his family. There's a story that they were actually already living in the hotel and Bemelmans offered to paint the mural because he was broke. "You know," says Tommy, "I'm here fifty-three years, and that's all I ever heard. So I don't know what to tell you."

14.

942 Madison Avenue
4 and 6 trains/77th Street

"DWELLINGS" ON MADISON AVENUE

Ruins for the little people

On a second-story window ledge of the old Mortgage and Trust Company building, you can spy what looks like a nest of clay: a red mound topped by a mysterious structure. A telephoto lens reveals that the structure is made from miniscule bricks and, very oddly, has the unmistakable stamp of human settlement. It could be an abandoned home for Southwest Indians – Hopi or Zuni – if they were only an inch tall.

The miniature ruins are the work of artist Charles Simonds. "For the past three years I've been going around the streets of New York," he says in a 1972 film about his structures, "building dwelling places for an imaginary group of Little People who are migrating through the city. Each dwelling tells part of the story of the life of these people." The dwelling visible from Madison Avenue is one of three in the same area; another can be seen tucked under the pyramidal roof of a chimney rising behind the Mortgage and Trust and the third is exhibited inside the Whitney Museum directly across the street. The attention of the museum anoints Simonds as a major American artist, but the project, begun downtown, really belongs on the street: the questions it raises – of security, community, change – are street questions. Embedding the clay structures in corners or on curbstones was how Simonds connected with New York: outside, under the eyes of neighborhood people. In the film we see him silently tweezering bricks the size of grains of rice to form tiny walls on a cement foundation in the Lower East Side, while onlookers try to figure him out. "Does he get paid for that?" asks one.

Simonds built each ruin with the idea that the action of the city would eventually wear them down to nothing: one less refuge for the little people. The piece on Madison, called "Dwellings", is naturally protected by elevation: the ledge and chimney structures have been here since 1981. The Mortgage and Trust is now tenanted by David Webb jewelers; employees can see the ruin in perfect detail – rough brick walls fortified by sticks – just outside the window of their small kitchen space. Saleswoman Alma Continanzi relishes the secret. "In this big city," she says, "here's this little corner that nobody would know."

15.

421 East 61st Street
mvhm.org
N, R, 4, 5 or 6 trains/59th Street – Lexington Avenue
F train/Lexington Avenue

MOUNT VERNON HOTEL MUSEUM

A last gasp of pastoral Manhattan

There are a handful of 18th- and 19th-century houses in Manhattan that create an illusion of stalled history: Dyckman Farmhouse, Morris-Jumel Mansion, Merchant's House. They all have creaking floors, a scent that is somewhere between polish and dust, and tables laden with wax food. The Mount Vernon Hotel is of this kind, with a difference. "After architectural historians came here," says Carol, a guide, "they determined that we are the only building still standing that operated as a day hotel."

If you don't know what a day hotel was, Carol says: "Think country club today." "Country" is exactly correct: although it now faces the humming Queensboro Bridge and is shadowed by the vaguely evil One Sutton Place North (a 40-story slab of black glass, it's been called the "2001 Monolith"), at the time of operation Mount Vernon was four miles into the boondocks. Urban New York City stopped at about 14th Street; those who could afford it would make the trip up the Boston Post Road in a carriage, or up the East River in a boat, to relax at this well-appointed stone carriage house. Upstairs the ladies sewed and sang; downstairs the men drank and played cards. The museum reveals curious aspects of the period. Novels are exclusive to the ladies' parlor, the men preferring newspapers. Water, generally foul at the time, is absent from the dinner table. The hotel was more than a place to take the air: it was a refuge from the cholera and yellow fever that burned through downtown.

Because the shift is frozen along with the history, Mount Vernon is the best site in the city to see the change, which hit Manhattan hard and fast, between traditional and modern city life. The dining room chairs are just beginning to show the uniformity of mass production. In the kitchen is a traditional hearth, but in front of it stands a more modern reflector oven. The parlor contains a harp, a pianoforte, and a flute, while in the corner squats a barrel organ, a machine that could play a short list of popular songs (No. 7: "Yankee Doodle"). In the 1820s, East 61st Street was a small and special dirt road. A generation later it would begin to lock with the grid.

The carriage house was built in 1799 and operated as a day hotel from 1827 to 1833. The land originally belonged to Col. William Smith and his wife Abigail Adams Smith, daughter of Founding Father John Adams.

op - Garden Concerts
MOUNT VERNON
1826
HOTEL.
MUSEUM

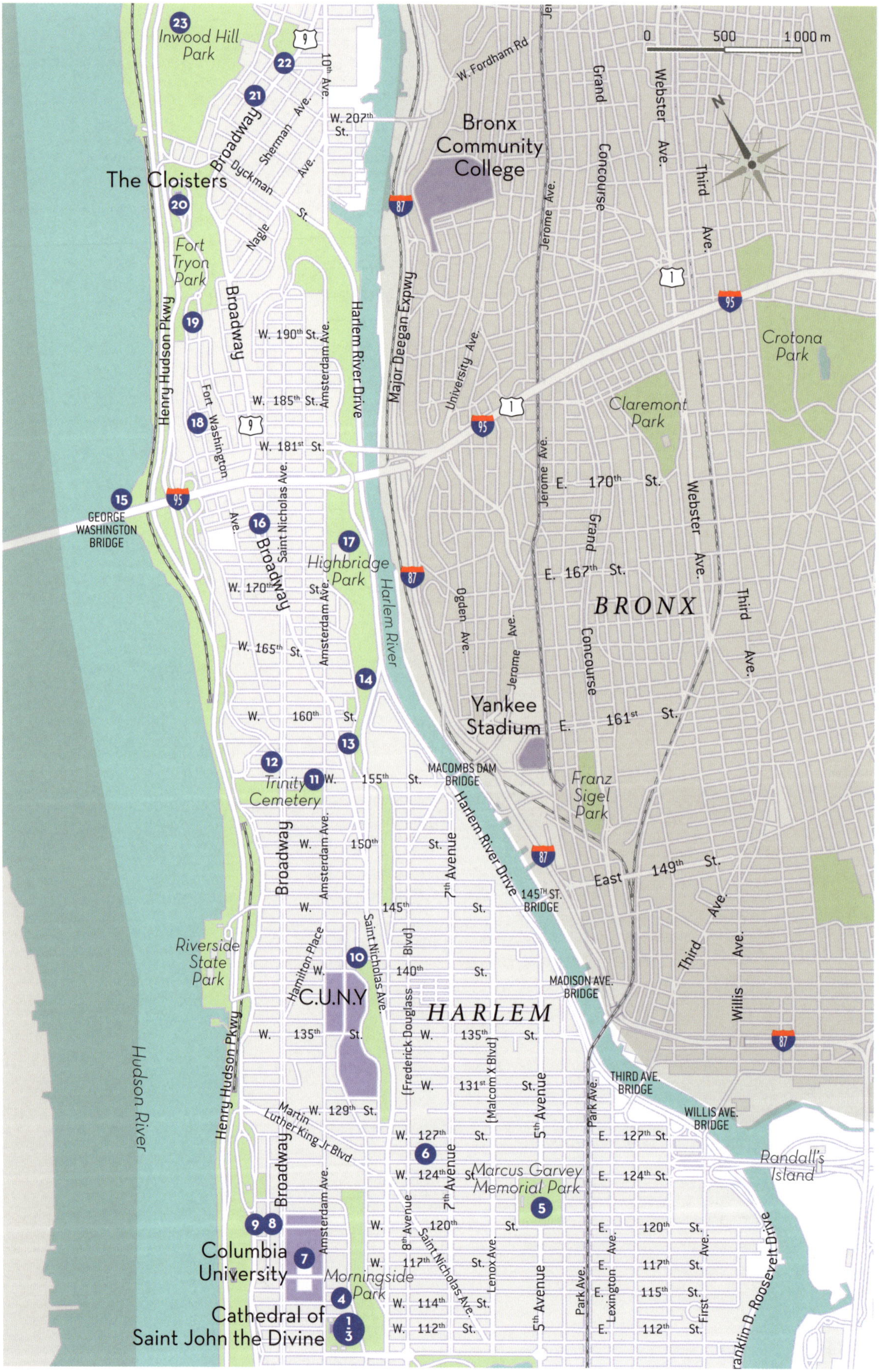
0
500
1 000 m
Inwood Hill Park
The Cloisters
Fort Tryon Park
Broadway
Sherman Ave.
Dyckman St.
Nagle Ave.
10th Ave.
W. 207th St.
W. Fordham Rd
Bronx Community College
Grand Concourse
Webster Ave.
Third Ave.
Jerome Ave.
Henry Hudson Pkwy
W. 190th St.
W. 185th St.
W. 181st St.
Fort Washington Ave.
Amsterdam Ave.
Harlem River Drive
Major Deegan Expwy
University Ave.
Crotona Park
Claremont Park
E. 170th St.
GEORGE WASHINGTON BRIDGE
Saint Nicholas Ave.
Highbridge Park
Harlem River
W. 170th St.
E. 167th St.
Ogden Ave.
BRONX
W. 165th St.
W. 160th St.
Yankee Stadium
E. 161st St.
MACOMBS DAM BRIDGE
Trinity Cemetery
W. 155th St.
Franz Sigel Park
W. 150th St.
7th Avenue
East 149th St.
W. 145th St.
145TH ST. BRIDGE
Riverside State Park
Hamilton Place
W. 140th St.
(Frederick Douglass Blvd)
MADISON AVE. BRIDGE
C.U.N.Y
HARLEM
W. 135th St.
Willis Ave.
Hudson River
W. 131st St.
(Malcom X Blvd)
5th Avenue
Park Ave.
THIRD AVE. BRIDGE
WILLIS AVE. BRIDGE
W. 129th St.
Martin Luther King Jr Blvd
W. 127th St.
E. 127th St.
W. 124th St.
Marcus Garvey Memorial Park
E. 124th St.
Randall's Island
W. 120th St.
E. 120th St.
8th Avenue
Columbia University
W. 117th St.
E. 117th St.
Lenox Ave.
Morningside Park
W. 114th St.
Lexington Ave.
E. 115th St.
First Ave.
Cathedral of Saint John the Divine
W. 112th St.
E. 112th St.
Franklin D. Roosevelt Drive

UPPER MANHATTAN

01.

Cathedral Church of St. John the Divine
Amsterdam Avenue and 112th Street
stjohndivine.org
1 train/110th Street – Cathedral Parkway

THE PORTALS OF PARADISE

New York: the big apocalypse

The Cathedral Church of St. John the Divine is unfinished, but it's already the biggest cathedral in the world. "Actually," says humble Al Blanco, a volunteer greeter, "I like to say that it's more or less the biggest in the world." Cologne Cathedral is higher, and the one in Seville is wider, and St. Paul's in Rome, while more massive, is not a cathedral at all but a basilica. It doesn't matter: St. John the Divine is awesomely huge, and pacing its insides is one of the most transporting architectural experiences New York has to offer. "People are just taken away by the size," Blanco says, "and the feeling that size gives." You have to wonder what feelings the designers wanted to give with the frightening carvings that decorate the front door.

The Portals of Paradise, the array of limestone sculptures that frame the cathedral entrance, were completed in 1997. Of the many biblical figures portrayed, seven – Isaiah, Jeremiah, Ezekiel and Daniel; Amos, Hosea and Jonah – are prophets. If prophets share one thing, it's a sweet tooth for carnage. Ezekiel stands on grimacing skulls, a nod to his Dream in the Valley of Dry Bones and representing, according to the cathedral brochure, "total destruction." The capital under Amos and Hosea shows a bus full of unlucky commuters hurtling off a broken Brooklyn Bridge. But it's the stonework between these two that many find most chilling. "New York City," reads the brochure, "including the Twin Towers, is portrayed under a mushroom cloud." The Towers are pitched for a fall, and couched in roiling flame.

Scaring folks into church is as old as God, of course. And it's worth noting that the whole cathedral is named after the author of the nutty "Book of Revelation". Still, many have deciphered sinister intent in St. John the Divine. It's been called Masonic, pagan, Satanic – if you squint hard enough, you'll find it here. But if the building makes some uncomfortable, it's less due to a wicked cabal than the clash that naturally results when a medieval colossus, complete with medieval stagecraft, is constructed in the 20th century – and on into the 21st.

02.

Cathedral Church of St. John the Divine
Amsterdam Avenue and 112th Street
stjohndivine.org
1 train/110th Street – Cathedral Parkway

BLESSING OF THE BICYCLES

You are performing a good work

Throughout the year St. John the Divine hosts events that some have complained are unchurchly. The criticism is less an indictment than a signal that where special programs are concerned, the cathedral gets New York. It gets the zombie-lovers who attend the Procession of the Ghouls every Halloween, and the pet owners who bring their dogs, cats, birds, ferrets, llamas, elephants, etc. to the yearly Blessing of the Animals, and the cyclists who roll their bikes into the church every spring for the Blessing of the Bicycles.

There are thousands of brave cyclists in the Death Race of New York City streets, and not all of them escape unscathed. In 1998, Glen Goldstein, the organizer of the Blessing of the Bicycles, approached St. John the Divine's leadership to see if some ceremony might be held in the interest of bicycle safety. The church gladly offered to allow bikes in the cathedral for a blessing with holy water. It's the kind of arrangement that would grate on the less tolerant: the cathedral is Episcopal, Goldstein is Jewish, and attendees are what-have-you (the event website: "Regardless of your religious beliefs – or lack thereof – you are welcome.").

More come every year. Led by a trio of bagpipers (one of them in Lycra), hundreds of cyclists wheel their rides through the cathedral's sculpted portico to the polished stone central aisle, forming orderly rows. The atmosphere is more comradely than solemn or even reverent. And though it's likely more bikes than you've ever seen under any roof, let alone a church roof, the Gothic enormity of the cathedral sweeps awesomely all around with room to spare, and the words of Reverend Tom at his podium rebound with echoes. "Whether you cycle for recreation or sport," hums the reverend, "whether you commute to work, or for whatever reason you cycle...or roll in any way that does not involve internal combustion ... you are performing a good work." When the speech is over, a shimmering chorus wells up as the cyclists, following an unspoken cue, ring their bells in unison.

The first recorded traffic accident in American history happened in New York, and involved a bicycle. Henry Wells lost control of his horseless "wagon" on upper Broadway, "going in a zig-zag fashion" until he knocked Evylyn Thomas off her bike. She survived.

BELOVED SON HEAR HIM
FRIDAY

03.

Cathedral Church of St. John the Divine
Amsterdam Avenue and 112th Street
stjohndivine.org
1 train/110th Street – Cathedral Parkway

"THE PEACE FOUNTAIN"

A puzzling battle of good versus evil

No surprise that the Cathedral of Saint John the Divine – peculiar in its own right – plays host to the weirdest public statue in New York City. The 40-foot-high "The Peace Fountain" is a heap of wild imagery: twisting flames, giant crustaceans, a DNA helix, a smirking moon, the severed head and nervous system of Satan, lovesick giraffes. Rising from the center is a gaunt Archangel Michael with a broadsword.

Two tourists take a stab at interpreting it:

"It's basically a guy with wings making out with a giraffe. And somehow Lucifer got his head ripped off by that ... whatever that is."

"Some kind of lobster. But that other part looks like shark teeth. I guess if you put it in a public fountain, it's just art."

"It's all art, dude."

Coded messages are nothing new in Christian statuary, and churches in medieval France, where St. John the Divine takes many of its cues, used demons and the damned for decoration. "The Peace Fountain" has been criticized for its vaguely pagan flavor, but Christianity is full of second-hand paganism, and anyway the gibe "Pagan!" has never had much impact in New York. So while the sculpture may not please everybody, it's definitely in the right place. But what does it mean?

For those who take the time to look, there's a convenient bronze plaque that explains everything – perhaps a little too explicitly. The fountain traces the continuity of life in the cosmos along a theme of good triumphing over evil. Giraffes, "among the most peaceable of animals," are good. The crab "reminds us of life's origins in the sea," and DNA is life's "key molecule." Greg Wyatt, the sculptor-in-residence of St. John the Divine, created "The Peace Fountain" in the cathedral's crypt. It was installed in 1985 and has been inspiring, offending, and baffling people ever since.

In counterbalance, the fountain is ringed by dozens of smaller bronze sculptures with inspiring messages from across the whole spectrum of spirituality: Aesop, Gandhi, John Lennon.

These smaller works were created by local schoolchildren. It might take more than that, though. While the tourists debate aesthetics, a group of first-graders troop down Amsterdam. One boy freezes, and fixes a leery eye on the fountain until his schoolmate tugs him back into line.

04.

405 West 114th Street
ccnd-nyc.org
1 train/Cathedral Parkway or 116 Street – Columbia University
A, B and C trains/Cathedral Parkway or 116 Street

CHURCH OF NOTRE DAME

A French cave, plus benefits

If you like a touch of theme park with your religious architecture, Notre Dame near Morningside Park has an unexpected attraction: the entire wall behind the altar has been sculpted to look like the interior of a cave. Not just any cave, but the famous grotto of Lourdes in southern France, complete with stone face, crawling ivy, and a niche for a statue of the Virgin.

It's natural for this church to have a marked French influence: Notre Dame was built as a chapel for the Fathers of Mercy, a community of French Catholic missionaries. The link to the grotto of Lourdes is owed to Estelle Livingston Redmond, a prominent Catholic from one of New York's oldest families, who purchased the land and financed the church's construction with the provision that it promote devotion to Our Lady of Lourdes, a manifestation of the Virgin Mary that was first reported at the French cave in 1858. Redmond believed that the natural spring water at Lourdes had healed her own son. The parish was officially affiliated with the French shrine in 1913, enabling worshippers – according to a process that the Roman Catholic Church presumably understands – "to obtain the same spiritual benefits as pilgrims who travel to Lourdes, France."

This affiliation stretches further than you think – all the way to the afterlife, in fact. In 2008, on the 150th anniversary of Mary's appearance, Pope Benedict XVI decreed that a pilgrimage to Lourdes on its jubilee year was worth a plenary indulgence – a kind of get-into-Heaven-free card.

During the week corresponding to the Virgin's first apparition (February 2–10), faithful Catholics could visit "in any church, grotto or decorous place, the blessed image of that same Virgin of Lourdes, solemnly exposed for public veneration" and have their stay in Purgatory reduced to zero. During that week, you could catch a Knicks game, see "The Lion King", and save your immortal soul all in the same town.

Today, the Church of Notre Dame continues its spiritual link to the grotto in France: it's an outlet for Lourdes water. "I would like __ bottles of Lourdes water" reads an order stub attached to the visitor pamphlet. "(I enclose an offering of $ __ to cover the cost of shipping.)"

According to a worker at the chapel: "It comes from France in containers, and then we put it in these little bottles."

AVE MA

05.

Marcus Garvey Park
2 and 3 trains/125th Street

HARLEM FIRE WATCHTOWER

The last of the first skyscrapers

On the top of a hill at the highest point of Marcus Garvey Park stands an old iron structure. If you ask around the neighborhood, you'll hear varying theories on what it was for. Slave market. Military fort. Lighthouse. "I know there's a big-ass bell up there," says one man. "That's about it." The big-ass bell weighs 10,000 pounds, and to understand its original purpose, you have to imagine a Manhattan where the buildings are at most five stories tall, and made of wood.

The Harlem Fire Watchtower on Mount Morris Hill, one of several iron watchtowers built during the same period, once commanded an uninterrupted view of the land around it.

Until the mid-1800s when the Croton Aqueduct began feeding fresh water into Manhattan (see page 50), fires were frequent and catastrophic. Older watchtowers were built of wood, and sometimes had an unfunny knack for catching fire along with everything else. In the 1840s an alternative was found, and with it the architectural key that would soon set the Manhattan skyline soaring. While on a trip to Italy, the engineer and inventor John Bogardus had the idea that the richness of ancient architecture could be reprised in cast iron. Structural iron had been used sparsely in small bridges and lower structures, but the cost remained prohibitively high. Bogardus took advantage of cheaper and more readily available iron, and the strength of interlocking cast beams. The system he conceived for the watchtower distributed weight throughout a metal skeleton – the same system that makes modern skyscrapers possible.

When Bogardus built his first tower on 33rd Street and Ninth Avenue in 1851, it became the only freestanding iron-frame structure in America.

Another tower on Spring Street soon followed. Bogardus bid on the Mount Morris tower, but was beaten out by a rival who had the good sense to follow his innovative design. In all, nearly a dozen iron watchtowers were eventually built throughout Manhattan. As the city rose around them, these structures, which drew the blueprint for height, became obsolete. The Harlem Fire Watchtower is the only one left.

06.

Apollo Theater
253 West 125th Street
apollotheater.org
2, 3, B, C and D trains/125th Street

THE WISHING TREE

Rub the stump

The big acts that have crossed the Apollo Theater stage are countless. But so are the small ones: the unknowns, the would-have-beens, the newly discovered. On Wednesdays for over seventy years the Apollo has hosted "Amateur Night," where anyone can perform to a raucous crowd. Next to the wings, on its own pedestal, sits an unlikely object: a section of a tree stump. The Wishing Tree, according to Apollo tradition, must be rubbed for good luck before testing your talent onstage. The hopefuls have polished the wood to a shine. Some of them stepped into the lights, took up the microphone, and moments later became Whitney Houston, or Ella Fitzgerald, or James Brown. Others stayed who they were: just people. Still, the stump contains dreams. The theater's history echoes the history of Harlem. Originally a burlesque house, under the management of Jewish partners it became the first venue in New York to introduce Black performers to white audiences. "The way Black people danced," says historian and Apollo tour guide Billy Mitchell, "the way we played our music, our theater, our poetry, our intellect, our activism – our whole swagger, as they say. Our white brothers and sisters wanted to see Black people perform." Once they did, they wanted more: American culture changed forever. And this wider success of Black culture inspired the unknowns of Amateur Night who took to the stage, rubbed the stump, and prayed for discovery.

The roots of the Wishing Tree go beyond the Apollo, and beyond the Harlem Renaissance, stretching deep into black city lore. The stump is one section of a great elm that grew on 131st Street, in front of the old Lafayette Theater, in the early 1900s the foremost African American venue in the country. Performers thought that standing in the tree's shade, or touching its bark or wearing its twigs and leaves would bring work, and luck. After the Wishing Tree was felled in 1934, pieces were sold off for souvenirs and firewood.

07.

Low Memorial Library, Columbia University
116th Street and Broadway
1 train/116th Street – Columbia University

THE HIDDEN OWL OF "ALMA MATER"

A sculptor with a thing for birds

On the steps of Low Library at the center of the Columbia University campus stands a statue most people know. "Alma Mater" has been the symbol of the school for over a century. Head ringed in laurel, 12 feet high, she raises her arms from her massive throne and surveys the quad with a bronze power stare, as though entranced by her own awesomeness. The grandeur is nicely offset by a quiet, secret detail: an owl that peers out from a hiding spot deep in the folds of "Alma Mater"'s gown.

The owl has a thematic logic behind it. "Alma Mater" symbolizes the cultivation of the student mind (in Latin the name means "nurturing mother"), but the figure is actually Minerva, Roman goddess of wisdom and war, and her mythical companion is the owl Glaucus. The owl's night vision makes it a natural sage: the eyes cut through the darkness. The work is a trove of other symbols: the gown represents academics, lamps swirling from the armrests are labeled *Doctrina* (learning) and *Sapientia* (knowledge), the scepter in *Alma Mater*'s right hand is topped with the crown of King's College, a reminder that Columbia began as a Royalist college (1754).

You might think: the other hand would make an excellent perch for an owl with night vision. But then it would be in the service of the institution. The owl is so hard to find, it connects to the very personality of the sculptor, Daniel Chester French: when you finally spy it, it's like receiving a secret handshake that spans decades. French was fascinated with birds; his first love was not art, but taxidermy. As a youth he was described as "of sunny disposition, bright and witty [...] but by no means decided as to his future work," and his earliest sculptural success was a pair of owls. He went on to become perhaps the greatest American sculptor of his time (it's enough to say: Lincoln Memorial).

There are dozens of Daniel Chester French works in New York City, among them the Four Continents on the steps of the Customs House (now the National Museum of the American Indian).

THE STATE OF NEW YORK
HERISHED FROM GENERATION TO GENERATION
HE GLORY OF ALMIGHTY GOD
A UNIVERSITY
MDCCCXCVII
ALMA MATER

08.

490 Riverside Drive
trcnyc.org
1 train/116th Street – Columbia University

RIVERSIDE CHURCH CARILLON

The heaviest tuned bell in history

Riverside Church, the tallest church in the U.S., was designed and built like a skyscraper. The stone hangs on a steel cage; construction, funded by John D. Rockefeller, began in 1927 and was completed only three years later. The sturdy frame does more than support the tons of ornamented masonry: inside the tower is the world's biggest carillon. The bass bell that marks the hour, the Bourdon, is the single heaviest carillon bell in history.

Although regular visits to the bell tower and the observation deck are a tourism casualty of 9/11, it's still possible, with persistence, to arrange a special tour with the visitor center. But the best way to see the tower is to accompany Ralph, the assistant maintenance engineer, while he does his daily check of the building. Ralph is a large man in a permanently good mood; he makes noise as he walks – keys jingling, walkie-talkie crackling – but moves lightly up and down the corridors and stairs of the church he knows as well his own home. "I love this place," he says. "I'm proud to work here, and I'm sure Mr. Rockefeller would want us to share it."

The elevator stops at the twentieth floor; a small stair leads to the carillon and open air. The bells hang in a wash of white noise: distant traffic from the street far below, wind beating from the north, the rattling metal shutters of the observation deck above. The Bourdon – 20 tons of expertly tuned bronze – is on the lowest tier; around and above it are arrayed 73 increasingly smaller bells. The combined weight: over 100 tons. In the middle is a cubicle where the bells are connected by levers and pulleys to a system of bars laid out like a piano keyboard. Despite the enormity of the bells, the action of the clavier is almost instantaneous. "Look," Ralph says, touching the highest keys – and immediately a pair of pure notes peal out. "That one," he nods at the lowest key (and biggest bell), "you've got to put a little more force into."

Here to make a regular checkup of the carillon is John Witkowiak. "They're the best bells I've ever heard," he says with an expert's bluntness. Witkowiak, a third-generation carillon caretaker, notes the tower's size. "Massive beams," he says. "Everything's riveted." Suddenly it's 1 o'clock, and the place goes crazy: the bells make your bones vibrate. Witkowiak, undaunted – or mostly deaf by now – turns around and gets back to work.

09.

490 Riverside Drive
trcnyc.org
1 train/116th Street – Columbia University

RIVERSIDE LABYRINTH

Still mysterious after a thousand years

On the floor of the Riverside Church chancel you'll find an interesting hallmark of the building's medieval roots: a stone labyrinth.

Labyrinths first started appearing in the floors of Christian churches (although they predate them) around the year 1000. One theory holds that meandering along the loops and switchbacks served as a proxy journey for devout Christians who couldn't make the pilgrimage to Jerusalem: the hassles of travel in a conveniently concentrated form. If bumping around a maze sounds like a surer path to rage than to spiritual fulfillment, keep in mind that labyrinths are patterns, not puzzles. Everyone who walks the labyrinth walks the same inevitable route: there's only one.

Completed in 1930, Riverside Church is modeled after Chartres Cathedral in France and inherited the labyrinth along with the architecture. Chartres has the most well-known church labyrinth in the world: over 40 feet in diameter, it fills the entire nave of the cathedral. The design in the floor of Riverside is mostly symbolic: formed by contrasting polished marbles, it's only 10 feet across – borderline unwalkable. Still, since the 1990s the church has attracted labyrinth enthusiasts with a larger, portable version that can be spread out on the floor. The practice began with Riverside Church member Richard Butler, who first helped create a paper labyrinth for Easter Holy Sunday, and later had the design painted on canvas. "I experience a clearing of my mind," Butler told the Times about walking it.

Labyrinths are a wider phenomenon. Diana Carulli, an artist who has designed large public labyrinths in Union Square and other parts of the city, says there's a growing public need for walking around in circles. "Labyrinths go through these tremendous revival periods," she says. "They work through strengthening your core in some mysterious way."

Riverside's Parish Life Ministry hosts labyrinth walks on a more or less quarterly basis. Anyone can come and try it.

10.

414 West 141st Street
nps.gov/hagr
1 train/West 137th Street
A, B, C and D trains/145th Street

HAMILTON GRANGE

A New York home for a Founding Father

Of all the Founding Fathers, Alexander Hamilton is the striver, the go-getter, meritocrat – the New Yorker. Born in the West Indies, he arrived a poor orphan, and within five years was personal aide to George Washington. He had a sixth sense for finance, and his concession to Thomas Jefferson – moving the nation's political capital to Washington D.C. but maintaining New York as the banking center – resounds even today. It follows that the man left traces in the city. You can raise a glass at Fraunces Tavern where he kept his first offices as United States Treasurer or visit the site of the oldest bank in the country, which he founded. You can stand on West 42nd Street and look just over the Hudson to Weehawken, where Hamilton dueled with Aaron Burr – or at the foot of his grave at Trinity Church. A surprising number of New Yorkers, especially those who see everything above 110th Street as a kind of exotic hinterland, are unaware that his last and only home is here, too.

Hamilton named the house the Grange after his grandfather's estate in Scotland. Part of why it's often ignored is a years-long restoration, finished in the fall of 2011. Then there's the unsettled character of the house itself: it has been moved – the entire thing – twice over the years, once four blocks west to a tight fit next to St. Luke's Episcopal Church (where a bronze statue of Hamilton still stands) and more recently to West 141st Street where the house was reoriented so it would better fit against St. Nicholas Park.

Hamilton's reasons for building this country home were chiefly parental. He had seven children in 1802 when the Grange was finished, and the long distance from New York – at that time almost completely contained in what we'd call downtown today – meant less risk from the city plagues of cholera and yellow fever. The house is small but comfortable: Hamilton called it his "sweet project," and likely saw himself dying there, old and content. Instead, he walked out early in the morning on July 11, 1804, to meet the Vice President of the United States in the country's most famous duel.

11.

Trinity Mausoleum and Cemetery
770 Riverside Drive
trinitywallstreet.org/cemetery-mausoleum
A and C trains/155 Street
1 train/157 Street

AUDUBON'S GRAVE MARKER

Bird killer (and painter)

Although the Washington Heights area offers some clues – Audubon Terrace, Audubon Avenue – the fact that "America's greatest naturalist" John James Audubon made a home here is news to many people. Audubon might as well be a myth: he seems to have lived in some harmonious and colorful dimension inhabited chiefly by birds. But the man died a New Yorker. Born in Haiti, raised in France, American by citizenship, Audubon spent years in thankless toil and poverty trying to create a perfect thing: a complete visual record of America's avifauna. When the project finally won him the fame he deserved, the painter bought an estate above 155th Street and lived there until his death in 1851.

The land of Trinity Cemetery was once part of this Audubon estate, and the naturalist's grave is one of the most impressive you'll find there: a 7-ton Celto-runic cross carved from a solid block of bluestone, 19 feet tall and covered with birds. Give it a careful look and you'll discover an aspect of the naturalist's career that most people would never suspect. On one flank of the stone base appear bas-relief painter's tools – palette, brushes, and maulstick – framed by leafy sprigs and flowers. But on the other side you'll find a powder horn, game bag and crossed hunting rifles. Audubon was by necessity an ace hunter first and an artist second: he killed pretty much every bird he ever painted. You almost can't find a portrait of the man where he's not holding a gun. He shot the birds, arranged them in vivid poses with the help of twisted wires, backdropped them with a grid to correct proportion, and then took his time with the art.

"BIRDS OF AMERICA"

Audubon's "Birds of America", first printed in 1827, contains almost five hundred different birds, including several species that have since gone extinct – the great auk, the pinnated grouse. When the man died, he left his estate to his wife, who had largely supported him while he tramped for years through America's backwoods. When the widow fell on hard times she sold the book's original watercolors to the New-York Historical Society for $2,000. Most of the copper plates for the engravings ended up melted at a scrap dealer. At a London Sotheby's auction in 2010, a complete edition of Birds of America became the most expensive printed book in history when it sold for $11.6 million.

AUDUBON.

12.

The Hispanic Society of America
Broadway between West 155th and West 156th Streets
hispanicsociety.org
1 train/157th Street
C train/155th Street

PORTOLAN CHART

America, *terra incognita*

If there's anything more compelling than a map of the world, it's an ancient map where things are patchy and strange, and whole continents of *terra incognita* fade off into the margin.

The Hispanic Society of America Museum has one hidden away in the library: a giant portolan chart on parchment from 1526 by Juan Vespucci, nephew of the great Italian explorer Amerigo.

Created for the purposes of trade, the portolan charts are the first no-nonsense maps of the known world. The one in the Hispanic Society is believed to be the official Spanish exploration atlas called the *padrón real*, or royal register. "When sailors returned from America to Spain," says library curator William Delgado, "they had to draw the contours of the coast that they saw, and make a report." The resulting chart, regularly updated, was a state secret: the New World glimmered in the imaginations of contending European powers like a vast tract of solid gold. The person in charge of compiling the fresh information was called the *piloto mayor* or "master navigator". The explorer Amerigo Vespucci held the title until his death in 1519, when it fell to his nephew Juan. The master navigator had to perform a political balancing act: both correctly record the buzz of new discovery and keep a lid on it. At some point, Juan tripped. "He got fired," Delgado smiles, raising his eyebrows at the 500-year-old scandal.

Vespucci's map still has an appealing air of secrecy about it. For one, it isn't kept in the main museum, but in the attached library. There you have to whisper your desire to an assistant, who will direct you to a curtained wall and, with a certain drama, pull the cord to reveal the known world of half a millennium ago. Europe is well-defined. Africa too, but the blocky elephants were drawn by someone who had clearly never seen one. Brazil is patrolled by mysterious dragons. Most striking is the nascent accuracy of the Americas: the Gulf of Mexico and the Indies are precisely drawn, and Florida appears as a peninsula and not the island it was once believed to be. As you would expect from a chart made by sailors, the details are in the coasts. Inland America grows vague: just a wash landscape of gloomy blue hills that fade into nothing, the very depiction of the unknown.

13.

Coogan's Bluff
at Edgecombe Avenue and West 158th Street
1 train/157th Street
A and C trains/155th Street

BRUSH STAIRWAY AND OLD POLO GROUNDS

The last trace of Manhattan baseball

An iron stairway on Coogan's Bluff once looked over the New York Giants baseball field, the Polo Grounds. Hidden behind teetering fences, half-buried in dead leaves, and leading nowhere, the Brush Stairway speaks as clearly as a gravestone: Manhattan baseball is long gone.

Baseball was born here. In fact Manhattan is woven into baseball's very geometry: the diamond came about in Madison Square in the 1840s, where office clerks began playing after work. The original game (called "rounders") had five bases, but the square was too small so they took one out and made it four. New York's first team, the Knickerbockers, codified the rules of the game in 1845, and baseball madness quickly followed: within a decade the sport was declared the national pastime.

So many fans came out for the first Polo Grounds game, hundreds couldn't get in. According to James D. Hardy's "The New York Giants Baseball Club", they "climbed to the top of Coogan's Bluff and watched from there, a site that promptly acquired the name of dead-head hill." This bluff remained a favorite place to catch a free game throughout the Polo Grounds' career until the field was demolished in 1964. In addition to the Giants, the stadium was also home to the Yankees and the Mets for shorter periods, and site of "The Shot Heard 'Round the World," Bobby Thomson's immortal homer against the Brooklyn Dodgers.

Today all that's left of the ball field is this stairway creeping down the bluff, and an iron message laid in the concrete landing by Giants owner John T. Brush. Standing there you can see the traffic along Harlem River Drive where Dominican taxi drivers park and gather around a food van. One of the older drivers remembers watching games from dead-head hill. "Sure," he says. "If you can't buy a ticket, you go right up there." He turns around to look over the drive at the identically dismal brick projects that now occupy the stadium's spot. "Long time ago." When asked if the food at the van is any good, he makes a friendly scowl: "Not really" – and then drives off.

This is the second site of the Polo Grounds; the first was on 110th Street and was in fact originally used for polo.

THE
JOHN T. BRUSH
STAIRWAY
RESENTED BY THE
NEW YORK
GIANTS'

14.

Highbridge Park
At the request of the artist, the exact location can't be printed here
The petroglyphs are incised into the north face of an outcrop of schist rock in Highbridge Park, between Edgecombe Avenue and Harlem River Drive, south of 165th Street
A and C trains/163rd Street – Amsterdam Avenue

MANHATTAN PETROGLYPHS

The antidote to Instagram

A petroglyph is an image created in relief on a stone surface by scraping or carving. A Paleolithic man in the year 30,000 BCE gouges the outline of a horse into the wall of a cave with a bear's rib bone: that's a petroglyph. A guy from Minnesota with a masters degree in fine art chisels a helicopter into a rocky outcrop of upper Manhattan: that's ... a little different, somehow. Petroglyphs are a form that went out of fashion with the invention of writing. You don't expect to see new ones, particularly not here, and particularly not depictions of jet planes, hot air balloons, space shuttles, or satellites. The effect is distinctly odd, and it's hard to know what to do with it. Chalk up a victory to Kevin Sudeith, self-defined "petroglyphist," and perhaps vandal.

Sudeith has work all over, from California to Nova Scotia, on commissions and public art pieces. The petroglyphs in Manhattan are a personal riff, and to find them you need to climb rocks and whack through poison ivy and pokeweed. It's part of the attraction. Coming upon the carvings, most of which are small enough to cover with your hand, is a private ordeal. This art form doesn't share well. You have to go to the rock: the rock will not come to you. You could call it the antidote to Instagram. An experienced draftsman, Sudeith first glimpsed the potential of the petroglyph form while visiting Australia. He saw a wall of rock art there with layered images: one part thousands of years old, another depicting a European man on a horse. This collapsing of history clicked with him, and his goal since has been to create art that not only endures, but could also form a connection with a local person around the site. It's a way to be both timely and timeless. "The thing with petroglyphs," Sudeith says, "is they exist on their own terms. Once they're made, they don't need an art world to find an audience. It will come at some point. When exactly doesn't really concern me — now or in a hundred years, both work equally well. And if nothing happens, a petroglyph will just sit there quietly. But it's definitely *something*. It will keep being that regardless of me, or my career. And that's enough."

15.

Fort Washington Park
Riverside Drive at 179th Street
under the George Washington Bridge
nycgovparks.org/parks/fortwashingtonpark/highlights/11044
A train/181st Street
Follow the Henry Hudson Greenway from Riverside Drive

THE LITTLE RED LIGHTHOUSE

The master of the river

In the summer of 1951, traffic along Riverside Drive suddenly began to slow down when it hit a certain section at the foot of the George Washington Bridge: drivers pausing to get a glimpse of a cherry-red lighthouse. It had been announced that the lighthouse, a familiar sight on the banks of the Hudson River for thirty years, would soon be sold off for scrap iron. The resulting fuss was all over the papers.

Leading the fuss were children. Since 1942 they'd been emotionally bonding with the tower through a popular book, "The Little Red Lighthouse and the Great Gray Bridge" by Hildegarde Swift and Lynd Ward. The story is about a contented lighthouse, "round and red and jolly," that saves ships from the fogs and currents of a treacherous stretch of the Hudson. The lighthouse marvels at its own importance: "Why," it thinks to itself, "I am the MASTER OF THE RIVER." This much of the story is true: the Hudson had seen so many accidents in that area – where a spur of land called Jeffrey's Hook juts out – it had been marked by lanterns as early as 1889. When the 40-foot red lighthouse was constructed in 1921, its powerful lamp and fog bell saved lives and cargo.

Ten years later the George Washington Bridge opened. Next to the brilliantly lit metal behemoth, the lighthouse went from heroic to merely cute. This crisis of identity is the real subject of the children's story. "Very likely I shall never shine again," it thinks. "And it was VERY, VERY SAD." If you think an illustration of a weeping lighthouse is too silly to be touching, go find a copy of the book. Things end well: the huge, cold bridge assures the lighthouse that the ships still need him, and a storm soon proves the bridge right. In the huge, cold city, things were different. The little red lighthouse really had become obsolete: the Coast Guard announced its imminent sale for scrap, and kids lost their minds. One psychiatrist of the Citizen's Committee on Children said that the lighthouse had become a symbol of security, giving "reassurance that even though you are little in a big world you won't be annihilated." Children wrote letters, some even sent pocket change. And, in an act of almost wondrous compliance, the city listened. The Parks Department took over the lighthouse, spruced it up, and opened it to the public. It's the only lighthouse left on Manhattan.

16.

4140 Broadway at West 175th Street
unitedpalace.org
A train/175th Street
1 train/168th Street

LOEWS 175TH MOVIE PALACE

A spell of mysterious adventure

In the Golden Age of Hollywood, New Yorkers saw films in sumptuous movie palaces. Most of them have been demolished, or are falling to dust, or survive as no more than facades. Perhaps the greatest one ever built still stands, proud and enigmatic, on 175th Street.

When you first see it, you know you're looking at something rare, but the theater's style is unclassifiable. It's been called "Indo-Chinese," "Mayan Revival-Oriental," "Cambodian Neo-Classical."

Times reporter David Dunlap shotgunned the entire architectural dictionary at it with "Byzantine-Romanesque-Indo-Hindu-Sino-Moorish-Persian-Eclectic-Rococo-Deco." Outside it looks vaguely like an ancient temple. Inside the walls shimmer with gilt: goddesses, cherubs, elephants, deities.

The palace is considered the grandest offering by architect Thomas W. Lamb, who is not remembered for restraint. "His buildings were pretty sober until about 1927," says Craig Morrison of the Theater Historical Society of America. "Then all of a sudden: kablooey."

Lamb wasn't alone: for movie palace architects, crazy was the rule. "We sell tickets to theaters, not movies," said theater chain owner Marcus Loew. In 1924, Loew bought a controlling interest in Metro-Goldwyn-Mayer studios – in other words films were made to drive the venue business, not the other way around. Movie palaces became fantasies of distilled exotic, casting, in Lamb's own words, "a spell of mysterious adventure."

Today you can visit Loew's 175th, but you can't see a movie there. In 1969 the abandoned palace was bought by Frederick "Reverend Ike" Eikerenkoetter, who renamed it the United Palace Theater and repurposed the space as headquarters for his radio and television ministry.

Ike, who drove a different color Mercedes every day of the week, preached that poverty was the root of all evil, and made millions flogging a bland and shady method called "Thinkonomics." But the reverend is forever redeemed in the eyes of theater enthusiasts: "It's an absolutely beautiful restoration," says Morrison.

Ike died in 2009, but his church still holds open service on Sunday afternoons. The preacher delivers a feel-good sermon to the first four or five rows while all around, the ornate walls and balconies, and the high curved ceiling drawn from a dream of the Orient, gleam in the low light.

EXIT
EXIT

17.

High Bridge Park
Between West 155th and Dyckman Streets, Edgecombe and Amsterdam Avenues
nycgovparks.org/parks/highbridgepark
A train/175th Street
1 train/181st Street

TOP OF THE HIGH BRIDGE TOWER

Once a month, a guided tour all the way up

Most New Yorkers familiar with High Bridge Park know it only from the window of a rushing car: a 200-foot-high stone tower that suddenly comes and goes above the trees on Harlem Drive. Many never even get that close. And scarcely anyone knows that not only is the tower visitable, it's climbable: once a month, the urban rangers of the Parks Department unlock the door and offer a guided tour all the way to the top.

After spiraling up the iron stair to the observation level, you'll see stretched out before you the Harlem River valley, and beyond a surprisingly green Bronx. Directly below, the river is spanned by a relic of the Croton Aqueduct: the red brick stripe of High Bridge itself. This bridge, the city's oldest, was the last leg of the aqueduct's 40-mile journey to Manhattan (see page 50).

The bridge was off-limits for decades before re-opening in 2015. "Some of you born before the seventies may remember it as a place to throw rocks at the traffic down below," says today's urban ranger, Jerry Seigler. He wears the standard-issue hat and on his belt hang a walkie-talkie, a baton, and handcuffs. If anybody remembers, they keep quiet. Ranger Jerry leads the group down the steps again and out to where the old bridge meets the rocky hillside of High Bridge Park.

It unfolds that the guided tour extends to the whole of the riverfront, which is serviced by trails and unexpectedly wild: dense greenery of vines, mossy rocks, and tall trees. It also unfolds that Ranger Jerry is a well of information. He knows social history (in the 19th century the park was a favorite spot for horse buggy racing), geology (the bedrock we see on the surface formed miles below, millions of years ago), botany and/or alcohol (mugwort weed is a component of beer production), Indian hunting tricks (deer were driven into the river and drowned)... In fact, Ranger Jerry might know everything.

The group hikes down a shaded track of clay. Except for the gravel of broken glass underfoot, it could be Appalachia. "This is one of my favorite trees," the ranger says, leading the way to a giant London plane with a gaping hole in the trunk. "One day I found somebody living here." We wait for this "somebody" to turn out to be an adorable raccoon, but Ranger Jerry really means somebody: a homeless man with a leaning mattress, a battery-powered TV, and a shopping cart chained to a tree.

18.

Fort Washington Avenue and West 183rd Street
nycgovparks.org/parks/bennettpark
1 train/181st Street

BENNETT PARK

The highest natural landmass in Manhattan

The New York skyline is drawn in architecture: you can easily forget that the spires and rises of the vertical metropolis are just the icing on a titanic stonescape of underlying geology. Manhattan is mostly composed of two kinds of rock: schist – the ashy, glittering stone that you can see in the outcrops of Central Park – and marble, found only in the north at Inwood. The rock undulates along the length of the island, swooping down over a hundred feet deep in Midtown and climbing to a peak in Washington Heights at the small outcrop in the middle of Bennett Park. A plaque embedded there gives the exact elevation: only 265 feet above sea level.

Still, the hill had strategic advantages. In the summer of 1776, George Washington reconnoitered the site and ordered the construction of a fortification, "a kind of citadel." In the park you can still see, outlined in stone, the footprint of a five-bastioned earthwork that was called Fort Washington in the general's honor (and is the namesake of Washington Heights and Fort Washington Avenue). After a series of close calls and setbacks, the Americans were hemmed in by a combined force of Redcoats and Hessians that outnumbered them four to one. General Howe, the British commander, unhelpfully pointed this imbalance out. The Americans dug in anyway and waited for the attack.

It came on November 16. From his position on the opposite shore of the Hudson, Washington could peer up at the fort through his spyglass and see Hessians bayoneting Americans to death. "Such is my situation," he wrote, "that if I were to wish the bitterest curse to an enemy on this side of the grave, I should put him in my place, with my feelings." The battle was bloody, and decisive: the British occupied Manhattan until the war's end.

AMERICA'S FIRST SERVICE WOMAN

When Margaret Corbin, "the heroine of Fort Washington," received a military pension, she became America's first Service Woman. During the battle she helped her artilleryman husband until he was killed; she then shot the cannon herself. In nearby Holyrood Church there is a tablet honoring her.

Due to the same feature of geology, this part of Washington Heights is also the location of Manhattan's deepest subway tunnel. The lowest stop on the island: 181st St on the 1/9 line.

THE·HIGHEST
NATURAL·POINT
ON·MANHATTAN
265·05 FEET
ABOVE·SEA·LEVEL
U·S·C·&·G·S·DATUM

19.

701 Fort Washington Avenue
cabrinishrinenyc.org
A train/190th Street

MOTHER CABRINI SHRINE

The first American Catholic saint

Frances Xavier Cabrini, the first American citizen to be made a saint by the Roman Catholic Church, lies in this shrine in Washington Heights. The sight of a dead person under glass can make visitors uneasy.

"Oh, they're spooked out, some of them," says Rose, the shrine secretary. "There's her skeleton, and some skin. But that's not what makes you a saint. A saint is the *miracles* they do." Rose, a Puerto Rican woman with a good laugh balanced by a dry administrative edge, has worked at the shrine for seven years. "You become ... I won't say a counselor, but you listen to people's problems."

The problems the Mother Cabrini shrine specializes in are those of immigrants, and in this respect New York is her natural place. Cabrini understood immigrants because she was one. After founding an Order in her native Italy, she arrived in the city in 1889 with a group of sisters, landing in the notoriously squalid Five Points in the Lower East Side. The residence was filthy, loud, and skittered with pests: at night, one of the sisters would stay up to defend the others from rats. The Italians were widely viewed at that time as a variety of sub-human. "The field is so vast to do good for our poor Italians who are abandoned and very much looked down upon," Cabrini wrote. "They cannot bear the sight of [us]." Much of Cabrini's charity work focused on children: schools and orphanages. When asked to take up hospital duties as well she resisted until, as Rose tells it, she was visited in a dream by the Virgin Mary "who had her sleeves rolled up to 'do the work you don't want to do yourself.'" Rose widens her eyes with awe at a personal rebuke from the mother of Jesus. "So she said 'All right, all right.'"

In all, Cabrini founded more than 60 institutions, among them a medical center on 22nd Street (now closed). She became a U.S. citizen in 1909 and was canonized in 1946. In the papal brief the saint is formally recognized as "the heavenly patroness of immigrants."

Rose fingers through a stack of paper and pulls out a recent letter from a Dominican woman: she begs desperately for an early release from prison so she can rejoin her children. The letter is written directly to the saint and the tone is familiar, but Rose is the one who'll answer it.

Mother Cabrini isn't completely here: the unsqueamish Church divvied her up. The heart is in Rome, the head in Codogno.

20.

The Cloisters Museum
99 Margaret Corbin Drive, Fort Tryon Park
metmuseum.org/cloisters
A train/190th Street

THE LAVAUDIEU TORSO OF CHRIST

An antique scarecrow

An unassuming wooden torso of Christ hangs on a bare wall in The Cloisters Romanesque wing. Incomplete, scarred, and stained by the centuries, it must be one of the least noted among the museum's artworks. But the sculpture has an outrageous story that sums up with comic precision the whole tale and purpose of The Cloisters as a cultural institution.

"If you're looking for bizarre places that are really awe-inspiring," says a Cloisters docent, "this would be at the top of your list." The awe is owed to the thousands of works of medieval art; what makes it bizarre – and unique among American museums – is the layout. To visit The Cloisters is to stroll through a clever patchwork of authentic monastic architecture: tons of carved stone were shipped from Europe to create it. This period-specific exhibition space was the brainchild and passion of George Grey Barnard, an American sculptor who studied in Paris and amassed a heap of European art – the kernel of the present collection. He had a passion for medieval sculpture that was rare at the time. "Now we recognize it as something very interesting," says the docent, "but it wasn't always so."

If the States were cool on the Middle Ages, the attitude in France was practically hostile. During the French Revolution, the National Assembly took over church property and sold it to private citizens. Abbeys became farmhouses, chapels became barns, statues were crammed into the gaps of old walls. That's how the religious stonework of Europe made its way into an American collection: it was there for the taking.

The docent stands by the torso and pauses to linger on the specialness of its appeal – a build-up to the punch line. "There's a great sensitivity to the anatomy of the human figure: bone, muscles, pulling skin. It's extraordinary for the twelfth century, and it's long been recognized as a really rare find." Barnard came upon the ancient torso near the Lavaudieu abbey in the Auvergne region. "He bought it from a French family," the docent says, "that had been using it out in the field. Dressed up. As a scarecrow."

21.

Broadway and West 204th Street
dyckmanfarmhouse.org
A train/Dyckman Street or Inwood – 207th Street
1 train/207th Street

DYCKMAN FARMHOUSE

The last farmhouse on Manhattan

Where the trees block out the lampposts and the fire escapes, you can look up at the Dyckman Farmhouse on the corner of Broadway and West 204th Street and see the rural 18th century. Upper Manhattan was then nothing but farmsteads and quiet creeks, and the hidden remains of Indian villages. For over two hundred years this plain white house, the last real farmhouse on Manhattan, has been an unchanging island of the past. Built by William Dyckman in 1784, the house was never modernized on the assumption that it would be torn down sooner than later. In the early 1900s there was talk of moving it to nearby Isham Park, but descendants of William stepped in to keep the house where it stands and open it to the public.

Now the museum staff goes to extravagant lengths to keep the farmhouse frozen in time. The upstairs has been maintained as it was when the house was converted into a museum in 1915, while the downstairs parlor and sunken kitchen are as accurate for a period farmhouse as historians today can possibly make it. "Our concept of the past constantly changes," explained former director Susan De Vries. "Any historic house museum is going to be a layering of history, and we acknowledge that those layers are important."

If you can glimpse the past by squinting at the house from the outside, inside is a thorough time warp. The decorations and furniture have been restored or reproduced at great pains, and the closer you look, the realer it gets: on the table a hand of cards is fanned out next to a half-drunk glass of Madeira wine; Missus' knitting lies on a chair in the corner; from the wall ticks and chimes a period clock. Downstairs is a warm kitchen, with a fresh loaf of bread on the table and diced carrots waiting to be thrown in the pot. The Dyckman Farmhouse has stopped. The only thing missing is the Dyckmans. The only thing out of place is you, a curious ghost from the future.

Leading to the cellar kitchen there's a patch of rock foundation with what looks like a strange ideogram carved into the surface: three superimposed squares connected by lines. It's actually an ancient board game, Nine Man Morris, and might have been chiseled there for the Dyckman children.

22.

Isham Park, south entrance
Broadway and 211th Street
nycgovparks.org/parks/isham-park
1 train/207th Street

MILESTONE NO. 12

The silent sentinel

There is a strange red sandstone block embedded in the wall at the entrance of Isham Park. The only features setting it apart from the rough granite all around are the regular shape and the muddy color of its crumbling face. Millions pass the block, on foot or on wheels, without a pause: to them it's nameless. To New York historians it's a relic known as Milestone No. 12.

Milestones are unique and suggestive monuments. On the one hand they're humble rocks that bear one simple message in a series; on the other they can summon in an instant galloping horses and coach horns and clouds of romantic dust. They are also collectible. Manhattan is 14 miles long, and tracing the fates of the 14 original markers has lured many researchers into weedy roadsides and forgotten basements, and into the stacks and maps of libraries.

The original milestones were installed in 1769 during a project headed by deputy postmaster Benjamin Franklin, who realized a need for regular postage fees. Franklin crept, with an odometer of his own invention, along the road connecting New York and Boston. This colonial artery, called the Boston Post Road, had already been in use for a hundred years, but it was the markers that made it. "A road was regarded with dignity and respect," wrote milestone expert and Historical Society curator Richard J. Koke, "when it was lined with well-cut stones."

As streets widened and shifted with the evolving map of the city, the milestones were uprooted and forgotten. Many are gone for good; others have been rediscovered in private gardens, in landfill, embedded in the front steps of houses. No. 10 is in the New York Historical Society collection; No. 11 is at the Morris-Jumel Mansion; Nos. 13 and 14 are still lost.

No. 12 first stood on Post Road at 190th Street; in 1813 the distances were recalibrated when mile zero became the newly-completed City Hall and the stone was moved (and perhaps recut, no one knows).

The message chiseled into the face, "12 Miles from N.York," was probably blasted off by the potshots of vandals. Sometime in the 1800s the stone was placed in the retaining wall where it stands today: worn, wordless, ignored, and as old as anything you'll find in Manhattan.

23.

Inwood Hill Park
Between Dyckman Street, Hudson River and Harlem Ship Canal
nycgovparks.org/parks/inwoodhillpark
A train/Dyckman Street or Inwood – 207th Street
1 train/207th Street or 215th Street

INDIAN CAVES OF INWOOD HILL

Shelter in Manhattan's last great forest

Not counting herds of mastodons (see page 180), nothing is harder to square with the current state of Manhattan than the communities of American Indians who hunted here (bears, deer, turkeys) and fished here (especially oysters) and even, some historians have proposed, paddled canoes straight across the island by connecting rivers. But that was then. You can think of the urban development of Manhattan as a wildfire lit in the Battery in the 1620s that gradually crackled its way uptown before burning out just shy of the island's very northwestern tip. There stands Inwood Hill, Manhattan's last great forest, and the only place to imagine how the island appeared to the earliest New Yorkers, the Lenape.

Inwood Hill Park's main attraction as prehistoric Manhattan is the Indian Caves. Natural overhangs in the rocky ridge that leads down to the waterfront provided temporary shelter to camping Lenape, and in one spot the caves, which were once deeper than they are today, make a through-and-through around massive boulders. The first archeological work in the area was conducted in the late 1800s by two enthusiastic amateurs (the only category of archeologist at the time), William Calver and Reginald Bolton, who combed northern Manhattan for artifacts. Calver later wrote that the opportunities for fishing and game hunting, along with the natural rock shelters, made northern Manhattan "unmatchable in the features possessed for the accommodation of primitive life" – a judgment that has gone uncontested since.

One can marvel that the frenzy of urban development has spared not only a piece of American Indian history but also the original scenery. Tulip trees of stupefying height, forested hills alive with birds (tanagers, cardinals, hawks, and in winter even bald eagles) and, up in the winding trails, no trace of the modern world except for the tiny rumble of a passenger jet far overhead.

The word "Manhattan" is of Lenape origin, but the meaning is unclear. "Manna-hata" was recorded by Hudson's first mate Robert Juet in 1609, and a year later the name first appeared on maps. Possible translations include "island" (Lenape: *menatay*), "place to gather wood for making bows" (*manahatouh*), and the far-fetched "place of general inebriation" (*manahactanienk*).

It was September 1995 and Thomas Jonglez was in Peshawar, the northern Pakistani city 20 kilometres from the tribal zone he was to visit a few days later. It occurred to him that he should record the hidden aspects of his native city, Paris, which he knew so well. During his seven-month trip back home from Beijing, the countries he crossed took in Tibet (entering clandestinely, hidden under blankets in an overnight bus), Iran and Kurdistan. He never took a plane but travelled by boat, train or bus, hitchhiking, cycling, on horseback or on foot, reaching Paris just in time to celebrate Christmas with the family.

On his return, he spent two fantastic years wandering the streets of the capital to gather material for his first "secret guide", written with a friend. For the next seven years he worked in the steel industry until the passion for discovery overtook him. He launched Jonglez Publishing in 2003 and moved to Venice three years later.

In 2013, in search of new adventures, the family left Venice and spent six months travelling to Brazil, via North Korea, Micronesia, the Solomon Islands, Easter Island, Peru and Bolivia.

After seven years in Rio de Janeiro, he now lives in Berlin with his wife and three children.

Jonglez Publishing produces a range of titles in nine languages, released in 40 countries.

Atlas

Atlas of abandoned France
Atlas of extreme weather
Atlas of forbidden places
Atlas of geographical curiosities
Atlas of unusual wines

Secret Atlas

Paris - The secret atlas
Venice - The secret atlas

"Soul of" guides

Soul of Amsterdam
Soul of Athens
Soul of Barcelona
Soul of Berlin
Soul of Brussels
Soul of Detroit
Soul of Kyoto
Soul of Lisbon
Soul of Los Angeles
Soul of Marrakesh
Soul of Marseille
Soul of Milan
Soul of New York
Soul of Paris
Soul of Rome
Soul of Tokyo
Soul of Venice
Soul of Vienna

Photo books

Abandoned America
Abandoned Asylums
Abandoned Australia
Abandoned Belgium
Abandoned Churches: Unclaimed places of worship
Abandoned cinemas of the world
Abandoned France
Abandoned Germany
Abandoned Italy
Abandoned Japan
Abandoned Lebanon
Abandoned Spain
Abandoned USSR
Abandoned world – An AI-generated exploration
After the Final Curtain – The Fall of the American Movie Theater
After the Final Curtain – America's Abandoned Theaters
Baikonur – Vestiges of the Soviet space programme
Cinemas – A French heritage
Clickbait – A visual journey through AIgenerated stories
Forbidden France
Forbidden Places – Vol. 1
Forbidden Places – Vol. 2
Forbidden Places – Vol. 3
Forgotten France
Forgotten Heritage
Oblivion
Secret sacred sites
Venice deserted
Venice from the skies

"Secret" guides

Secret Amsterdam
Secret Bali – An unusual guide
Secret Bangkok
Secret Barcelona
Secret Bath – An unusual guide
Secret Belfast
Secret Berlin
Secret Boston – An unusual guide
Secret Brighton – An unusual guide
Secret Brooklyn – An unusual guide
Secret Brussels
Secret Budapest
Secret Buenos Aires
Secret Campania
Secret Cape Town
Secret Copenhagen
Secret Dolomites
Secret Dublin – An unusual guide
Secret Edinburgh – An unusual guide
Secret Florence
Secret French Riviera
Secret Geneva
Secret Glasgow – An unusual guide
Secret Granada
Secret Helsinki
Secret Istanbul
Secret Johannesburg
Secret Lisbon
Secret Liverpool – An unusual guide
Secret London – An unusual guide
Secret London – Unusual bars & restaurants
Secret Los Angeles – An unusual guide
Secret Louisiana – An unusual guide
Secret Madrid
Secret Mexico City
Secret Milan
Secret Montreal – An unusual guide
Secret Naples
Secret New Orleans – An unusual guide
Secret New York – An unusual guide
Secret New York – Curious activities
Secret New York – Hidden bars & restaurants
Secret Normandy
Secret Paris
Secret Potsdam
Secret Prague
Secret Provence
Secret Rio de Janeiro
Secret Rome
Secret Seville
Secret Singapore
Secret Sussex – An unusual guide
Secret Tokyo
Secret Tuscany
Secret Venice
Secret York – An unusual guide

Follow us on Facebook and Instagram

ACKNOWLEDGEMENTS

Summer Ash, Ana-Maria Lucaciu, Nelson Hancock, Lucien D'Azay, John Garrett, J.P. Bernbach, Ellen Adamson, Jason & Mari Tuttle, Mika Karlsson, Alex Ekman, Dave Arnold, Carl Mehling, New-York Historical Society library, Anisa Tejpar, Nicole Pangelinan, Lloyd Sandefur, Bob Stevenson, Jerry Seigler, Andy Young, Reggie Bolton, Bram Gunther, Chiara Barbieri, Saint Patrick's Cathedral, Connie Swierkowski, Rafael Balaguer, Columbia University Classics Department, Clancy Nolan, Mark Emanuel, Benjamin Tzafa, Matteo Pagani.

PHOTO CREDITS

All photos are by **T.M. Rives** except:
Alix Piorun: The Hess Spite Triangle, IFC Center's peepholes, The remains of Pier 54, The medallions of the Avenue of the Americas, Lenin on Norfolk Street, The crown on St. Paul's pulpit
Cover: © Jo Wiggijo on Pixabay

TEXTS CREDITS

All texts are by **T.M. Rives** except:
Hannah Frishberg: The Hess Spite Triangle, IFC Center's peepholes, The remains of Pier 54

Cartography: **Cyrille Suss** – Graphic design and layout: **Coralie Cintrat and Emmanuelle Willard Toulemonde** – Copy-Editing: **Caroline Lawrence and Sigrid Newman** – Proofreading: **Abigail Kafka** – Publishing: **Clémence Mathé**

Registration of copyright: October 2025 – Edition: 01
ISBN: 978-2-36195-817-6
Printed in Italy by L.E.G.O.